D1517884

THE **IRISH** KITCHEN

150 recipes for everyday
cooking from the Emerald Isle

CONTENTS

INTRODUCTION

It's called the Emerald Isle because its lush landscape glows a jewel-like green year round. Most Americans' experience with Irish cooking is limited to the ubiquitous salty corned beef, soggy cabbage, and leaden soda bread that shows up on our menus every St. Patrick's Day, but Ireland is a true culinary gem. Its moist weather, seaside geography, and mineral-rich land yield not just visually stunning vistas, but also a bounty of edibles that goes far beyond corned beef and cabbage. It is a cuisine that is at once rustic and refined, subtle, full of flavor, and varied. Most of all, it is based on the abundance of quality ingredients found here.

Although we tend to think of Irish cuisine as being heavily meat dependent—Irish stew, shepherd's pie, and corned beef being the most often cited representative dishes—Ireland boasts 3,500 miles of coastline and its seas are literally teaming with seafood. Salmon, trout, lobster, mussels, oysters, cockles, and other fish and shellfish are plentiful. Produce, too, is abundant and of superior quality. And its emerald pastures yield some of the world's best meat and dairy. Oysters plucked fresh from the sea, bubbling hearty soups and stews full of meat and vegetables, rich and buttery mashed potatoes studded with scallions, creamy cheeses, and moist, fresh-baked soda bread are the true trademarks of Ireland's cuisine. Indeed, although Irish cooking boasts hearty stews, tender greens, and fresh-baked breads among its notable dishes, the cuisine is far more than we've been led to believe.

As subtle and full of flavor as Irish cooking is, it is not difficult to reproduce, even for novice cooks. The techniques are those used for centuries by home cooks with the most basic appliances. What sets Irish cooking apart is not fancy techniques or rare ingredients, but the quality of its readily available local products.

The key to fantastic Irish cooking is to rely on high-quality ingredients—the best seasonal produce, local and organic meats, fish and seafood fresh from the sea, and high-quality dairy from pastured cows, sheep, and goats. Visit your local farmer's market, old-fashioned butcher, fish market, and cheese dealer to find the best-quality ingredients and you'll be on your way to feasting on fine Irish cuisine.

Irish cooking is loaded with classic dishes and regional specialties, with recipes perfected by generations of cooks. This book contains simple recipes for real Irish cooking, both traditional favorites and those with a contemporary twist. There are classic dishes favored by Irish grandmothers, such as Shepherd's Pie, Irish Soda Bread, Colcannon, and Irish Tea Cake. Comforting dishes perfectly suited to Ireland's cool climate include Luxury Cauliflower & Cheese, Beef and Stout Pies, and Potato Pancakes. A chapter on celebratory dinners offers impressive dinner party-worthy dishes, such as Glazed Ham in Cider, Pork Tenderloin with Roasted Rhubarb, and Roasted Goose with Apple Stuffing & Cider Gravy. The Perfect Desserts chapter delivers time-honored favorites, including Date Cake with Caramel Sauce, Irish Whiskey Trifle, and Irish Cream Cheesecake. The final chapter offers the best baked goods from any Irish oven: Lavender Shortbread, Rhubarb, Raisin and Ginger Muffins, Irish Spiced Fruitcake, Molasses Bread, Savory Oat Crackers, and more. Both inspiring and practical, this stunning book offers an exciting range of dishes. It will teach you how to quickly and easily prepare delicious, authentic, home-cooked meals true to the cuisine of the Emerald Isle.

INTRODUCTION

CLASSIC FAVORITES

HEARTY BEEF STEW

Serves: 4 **Prep: 35 minutes** **Cook: 2¼–2½ hours,** plus resting

Ingredients

3 pounds boneless chuck shoulder beef, cut into 2-inch pieces

2 tablespoons vegetable oil

2 onions, cut into 1-inch pieces

3 tablespoons all-purpose flour

3 garlic cloves, finely chopped

4 cups beef broth

3 carrots, cut into 1-inch lengths

2 celery stalks, cut into 1-inch lengths

1 tablespoon ketchup

1 bay leaf

¼ teaspoon dried thyme

¼ teaspoon dried rosemary

8 Yukon gold or red-skinned potatoes (about 2 pounds), cut into large chunks

salt and pepper

Method

1 Season the beef generously with salt and pepper. Heat the oil in a large flameproof casserole dish or Dutch oven over high heat. When the oil begins to smoke slightly, add the beef, in batches, if necessary, and cook, stirring frequently, for 5–8 minutes, until well browned. Using a slotted spoon, transfer to a bowl.

2 Reduce the heat to medium, add the onions, and cook, stirring occasionally, for 5 minutes, until translucent. Stir in the flour and cook, stirring constantly, for 2 minutes. Add the garlic and cook for 1 minute. Whisk in 1 cup of the broth and cook, scraping up the sediment from the bottom of the casserole, then stir in the remaining broth and add the carrots, celery, ketchup, bay leaf, thyme, rosemary, and 1 teaspoon of salt. Return the beef to the casserole.

3 Bring to a gentle simmer, cover, and cook over low heat for 1 hour. Add the potatoes, replace the lid, and simmer for 30 minutes. Remove the lid, increase the heat to medium, and cook, stirring occasionally, for an additional 30 minutes, until the meat and vegetables are tender. If the stew is too thick, add a little more broth or water and adjust the seasoning to taste. Let rest for 15 minutes before serving.

★ Variation

For extra flavour and colour garnish with fresh tarragon. Add some fresh tarragon for an extra delicious stew.

SHEPHERD'S PIE

Serves: 6   **Prep: 30 minutes**   **Cook: 1¼–1½ hours**

Ingredients

1 tablespoon olive oil

2 onions, finely chopped

2 garlic cloves,
finely chopped

1½ pounds ground lamb

2 carrots, finely chopped

1 tablespoon
all-purpose flour

1 cup beef or chicken broth

½ cup red wine

Worcestershire sauce
(optional)

salt and pepper

Mashed potatoes

6 russet or Yukon gold
potatoes (about
1½ pounds), cut
into chunks

4 tablespoons butter

2 tablespoons light cream
or milk

salt and pepper

Method

1 Preheat the oven to 350°F.

2 Heat the oil in a large saucepan and sauté the onion until softened, then add the garlic and stir well. Raise the heat and add the meat. Cook quickly to brown the meat all over, stirring continually. Add the carrots and season with salt and pepper to taste. Stir in the flour and add the broth and wine. Stir well and heat until simmering and thickened.

3 Put the meat mixture into a covered casserole dish or Dutch oven and cook in the oven for about 1 hour. Check the consistency from time to time and add a little more broth or wine, if required. The meat mixture should be thick but not dry. Season to taste with salt. Add a little Worcestershire sauce, if desired.

4 While the meat is cooking, make the mashed potatoes. Cook the potatoes in a large saucepan of lightly salted boiling water for 15–20 minutes. Drain and mash with a potato masher until smooth. Add the butter and cream, season with salt and pepper to taste. Spoon the lamb mixture into an ovenproof serving dish and spread or pipe the mashed potatoes on top.

5 Increase the oven temperature to 400°F and cook the casserole for an additional 15–20 minutes at the top of the oven, until golden brown. Serve immediately.

CLASSIC FAVORITES

IRISH SODA BREAD

Makes: 1 loaf

Prep: 20 minutes,
plus cooling

Cook: 25–30 minutes

Ingredients

vegetable oil, for oiling

3⅔ cups all-purpose flour, plus extra for dusting

1 teaspoon salt

1 teaspoon baking soda

1⅔ cups buttermilk

Method

1 Preheat the oven to 425°F. Oil a baking sheet.

2 Sift the flour, salt, and baking soda into a mixing bowl. Make a well in the center of the dry ingredients and pour in most of the buttermilk. Mix well together using your hands. The dough should be soft but not too wet. If necessary, add the remaining buttermilk.

3 Turn out the dough onto a lightly floured surface and knead it lightly. Shape into an 8-inch circle.

4 Place the loaf on the prepared baking sheet and cut a cross into the top with a sharp knife. Bake in the preheated oven for 25–30 minutes, until golden brown and it sounds hollow when tapped on the bottom. Transfer to a wire rack and let cool slightly. Serve warm.

APPLE & OATMEAL COOKIES

Makes: 26   **Prep: 30 minutes,** plus cooling   **Cook: 12–15 minutes**

Ingredients

2 large apples,
such as Granny Smith,
peeled and cored

1 teaspoon lemon juice

2 sticks butter, softened,
plus extra for greasing

½ cup firmly packed
light brown sugar

½ cup granulated sugar

1 egg, beaten

1¾ cups all-purpose flour

1¾ teaspoons
baking powder

1¾ cups rolled oats

½ cup raisins

Method

1 Preheat the oven to 350°F. Grease three large baking sheets. Finely dice the apples and toss in the lemon juice.

2 Put the butter, brown sugar, and granulated sugar into a bowl and beat together until creamy. Gradually beat in the egg. Sift in the flour and baking powder, then add the oats, raisins, and apple. Mix until thoroughly combined.

3 Place tablespoonfuls of the dough onto the prepared baking sheets, spaced well apart.

4 Bake in the preheated oven for 12–15 minutes, or until golden around the edges. Let cool on the baking sheets for 5–10 minutes, or until firm enough to transfer to a wire rack to cool completely.

CLASSIC CHOCOLATE CAKE

Serves: 8

Prep: 30–35 minutes,   Cook: 25–30 minutes
plus cooling

Ingredients

1¼ cups all-purpose flour

¼ cup unsweetened cocoa powder

¾ cup plus 2 tablespoons granulated sugar

1 tablespoon baking powder

1½ sticks unsalted butter, at room temperature, plus extra for greasing

3 eggs beaten

1 teaspoon vanilla extract

2 tablespoons milk

Frosting

1 stick unsalted butter, at room temperature

1⅔ cups confectioners' sugar

2 tablespoons unsweetened cocoa powder

1 teaspoon vanilla extract

Method

1 Preheat the oven to 350°F. Grease and line the bottom and sides of two 8-inch cake pans. Sift the flour, cocoa, sugar, and baking powder into a large bowl and make a well in the center.

2 Beat the butter until soft. Add the butter to the dry ingredients with the eggs, vanilla extract, and milk. Beat lightly with a wooden spoon until just smooth.

3 Spoon the batter into the prepared pans, smoothing with a spatula. Bake in the preheated oven for 25–30 minutes, until risen and firm.

4 Let the cakes cool in the pans for 2–3 minutes, then turn out onto a wire rack and let cool completely.

5 To make the frosting, beat the butter until smooth and fluffy. Sift the confectioners' sugar with the cocoa and beat into the butter until smooth.

6 Stir in the vanilla extract with enough hot water to mix to a soft spreading consistency.

7 When the cakes are cold, sandwich them together with half the frosting, then spread the remainder over the top, swirling with a spatula. Cut into slices and serve.

IRISH CHICKEN SOUP

Serves: 4   **Prep: 20 minutes**   **Cook: 35 minutes**

Ingredients

2 celery stalks, halved lengthwise and diced

4 small carrots, thinly sliced

1 small leek, halved lengthwise and sliced

3½ cups chicken broth

1 bay leaf

1 cup diced cooked chicken

½ cup shelled peas

4 small scallions, some green tops included, sliced

1 egg yolk

⅓ cup heavy heavy cream

4 small butterhead lettuce, shredded

salt and pepper

Method

1 Put the celery, carrots, and leek into a saucepan with the broth, bay leaf, and salt and pepper to taste. Cover and bring to a boil. Reduce the heat to medium, then simmer for 15 minutes, or until tender.

2 Add the chicken, peas, and scallions. Simmer for about 8 minutes, or until the peas are just tender.

3 Remove the pan from the heat. Lightly beat the egg yolk and cream together, then stir the mixture into the soup. Reheat gently, stirring.

4 Ladle into warm bowls, add the lettuce, and serve immediately.

MASHED POTATOES WITH SCALLIONS

Serves: 4   **Prep: 25 minutes**   **Cook: 30 minutes**

Ingredients

8 russet potatoes (about 2 pounds), cut into even chunks

20 scallions, some green tops included, chopped

1½ cups milk

¼ teaspoon white peppercorns

¼ cup snipped chives

1 teaspoon sea salt flakes

1 stick salted butter, melted and hot

Method

1 Add the potatoes to a large saucepan of salted boiling water, cover, bring back to a boil, and simmer gently for 20 minutes, until tender. Drain well and put back in the pan. Cover with a clean dish cloth for a few minutes to get rid of any excess moisture.

2 While the potatoes are cooking, put the chopped scallions into a saucepan with the milk and peppercorns. Simmer for 5 minutes, then drain, reserving the milk and scallions separately.

3 Mash the potatoes until smooth, stirring in enough of the reserved milk to produce a creamy consistency. Stir in the scallions and chives. Season to taste with sea salt flakes and more pepper, if necessary.

4 Transfer the potato mixture to a warm serving dish. Make a well in the center and pour in the hot, melted butter. Serve immediately, mixing in the melted butter at the table.

CLASSIC FAVORITES

SEEDED POTATO BREAD

Makes: 4 small loaves

Prep: 35–40 minutes   Cook: 1 hour 5 minutes

Ingredients

7 russet potatoes (about 1¾ pounds)

2 tablespoons salted butter, plus extra to serve

⅔ cup milk

2 teaspoons salt

½ teaspoon black pepper

1½ teaspoons dill seeds or caraway seeds (optional)

2¾ cups all-purpose flour, plus extra for dusting

1 teaspoon baking powder

Method

1 Preheat the oven to 375°F. Peel four of the potatoes, cut them into even chunks, and bring to a boil in a large saucepan of salted water. Cover and simmer gently for about 20 minutes, until tender. Drain well and put back into the pan. Cover with a clean dish cloth for a few minutes to get rid of any excess moisture. Mash with the butter until smooth.

2 Meanwhile, peel the remaining three potatoes and grate coarsely. Wrap in a clean piece of cheesecloth and squeeze tightly to remove the moisture. Put the grated potatoes in a large bowl with the milk, ¾ teaspoon of the salt, the pepper, and dill seeds, if using. Beat in the mashed potatoes.

3 Sift the flour, baking powder, and remaining salt onto the potato mixture. Mix to a smooth dough, adding a little more flour if the mixture is too soft.

4 Knead lightly, then shape into four flat, round loaves about 4 inches in diameter. Place on a nonstick baking sheet. Mark each loaf with a large cross. Bake in the preheated oven for 40 minutes, or until well risen and golden brown.

5 Break each loaf into quarters. Serve warm, spread with butter.

IRISH STEW

Serves: 4   **Prep: 25–30 minutes   Cook: 2½ hours**

Ingredients

¼ cup all-purpose flour

3 pounds boneless shoulder of lamb, trimmed of fat

3 large onions, chopped

3 carrots, sliced

4 Yukon gold or red-skinned potatoes (about 1 pound), quartered

½ teaspoon dried thyme

3½ cups hot beef broth

salt and pepper

2 tablespoons chopped fresh parsley, to garnish

Method

1 Preheat the oven to 325°F. Put the flour into a plastic bag and season well with salt and pepper. Add the lamb to the bag, tie the top, and shake well to coat. Do this in batches, if necessary. Arrange the lamb in the bottom of a casserole dish or Dutch oven.

2 Layer the onions, carrots, and potatoes on top of the lamb.

3 Sprinkle in the thyme and pour in the broth, then cover and cook in the preheated oven for 2½ hours. Garnish with the parsley and serve straight from the casserole.

MIXED FRUIT IRISH BREAD

Makes: 1 loaf

Prep: 30 minutes,
plus rising and cooling

Cook: 1 hour

Ingredients

4¾ cups white bread flour, plus extra for dusting

1 teaspoon allspice

1 teaspoon salt

2 teaspoons active dry yeast

1 tablespoon sugar

1¼ cups lukewarm milk

⅔ cup lukewarm water

vegetable oil, for oiling

4 tablespoons butter, softened, plus extra to serve

2 cups mixed dried fruit (golden raisins, currants, and raisins)

milk, for glazing

Method

1 Sift the flour, allspice, and salt into a warm bowl. Stir in the yeast and sugar. Make a well in the center and pour in the milk and water. Mix well to make a sticky dough. Turn out the dough onto a lightly floured work surface and knead until no longer sticky. Put the dough into an oiled bowl, cover with plastic wrap, and let rise in a warm place for 1 hour, until doubled in size.

2 Turn out the dough onto a floured work surface and knead lightly for 1 minute. Add the butter and dried fruit to the dough and work them in until completely incorporated. Return the dough to the bowl, replace the plastic wrap, and let rise for 30 minutes.

3 Oil a 9-inch round cake pan. Pat the dough to a neat circle and fit in the pan. Cover and let rest in a warm place until it has risen to the top of the pan. Meanwhile, preheat the oven to 400°F.

4 Brush the top of the loaf lightly with milk and bake in the preheated oven for 15 minutes. Cover the loaf with aluminum foil, reduce the oven temperature to 350°F, and bake for an additional 45 minutes, until golden brown and it sounds hollow when tapped on the bottom. Transfer to a wire rack and let cool.

CLASSIC FAVORITES

IRISH TEA CAKE

Serves: 8–10

Prep: 35–40 minutes, Cook: 1 hour
plus cooling

Ingredients

1½ sticks butter, softened, plus extra for greasing

1 cup superfine or granulated sugar

1 teaspoon vanilla extract or 1 vanilla bean, scraped

2 eggs

⅓ cup cream cheese

1¾ cups all-purpose flour, plus extra for dusting

1 teaspoon baking powder

¼ teaspoon salt

1 cup golden raisins

⅔ cup buttermilk

Glaze

⅓ cup confectioners' sugar, sifted

2 teaspoons fresh lemon juice

Method

1 Preheat the oven to 325°F. Grease a 9 x 5 x 3-inch loaf pan. Dust with flour and line the bottom with parchment paper. Put the butter, sugar, and vanilla extract into a large mixing bowl and beat with an electric mixer until fluffy. Add the eggs, one at a time, beating after each addition until combined.

2 Add the cream cheese and beat until well combined. Sift together the flour, baking powder, and salt into a separate bowl. Put the golden raisins into a small bowl. Add 3 tablespoons of the flour mixture to the golden raisins and stir until well coated. Gradually add the remaining flour mixture to the butter mixture, alternating with the buttermilk, and mix until smooth. Add the golden raisins and stir with a wooden spoon until well combined.

3 Transfer the batter to the prepared pan, smoothing the surface with a spatula. Bake in the middle of the preheated oven for about 1 hour, until golden, and a toothpick inserted into the center comes out clean. Remove from the oven and let cool in the pan for 10 minutes. Using a spatula separate the cake from the sides of the pan and transfer to a wire rack to cool.

4 Meanwhile, to make the glaze, combine the sugar and lemon juice in a small bowl and stir until smooth. Spread the glaze over the warm cake and let cool completely. Cut into slices and serve.

CLASSIC FAVORITES

CRAB IN CREAMY WHISKEY SAUCE

Serves: 2　　　　**Prep: 25 minutes**　　　　**Cook: 10 minutes**

Ingredients

2 large cooked crabs
2 tablespoons salted butter
1 shallot, finely chopped
¼ cup Irish whiskey
½ cup heavy cream
sea salt flakes
black pepper
pinch of cayenne pepper
pinch of paprika, to garnish (optional)

To serve

steamed baby carrots
steamed sea asparagus or peas

Method

1 Pull the claws and legs from the crabs and separate at the joints into sections. Crack with a mallet. Use a skewer or teaspoon to pick out the meat from all the sections except the claws. Set these aside. Pick out the meat from the body section, discarding the pointed gills (dead men's fingers), the stomach sac, and any sludgy brown sediment.

2 Melt the butter in a skillet over medium heat. Add the shallot and cook for 5 minutes, until soft. Add the crabmeat and the reserved cracked claws.

3 Pour in the whiskey and ignite it. When the flames die down, stir in the cream. Season to taste with sea salt, black pepper, and a pinch of cayenne. Stir for a few minutes, until heated through.

4 Divide between two warm plates. Garnish with a pinch of paprika, if using. Serve with lightly cooked baby carrots and sea asparagus or peas. Use your fingers to extract the crabmeat from the claws.

CLASSIC FAVORITES

Serves: 4–6   **Prep: 30 minutes**   **Cook: 1 hour 25 minutes**

Ingredients

1 pound bacon

8 good-quality
pork sausage links

4 onions, sliced

black pepper

1 leek, some green tops
included, sliced

2 bay leaves

2 sprigs thyme

¼ cup chopped fresh
parsley

2 garlic cloves, chopped

6 Yukon gold or red-skinned
potatoes (about 1½ pounds,
cut into 2 or 3 large chunks

3 cups ham broth or
chicken broth

soda bread, to serve

Method

1 Preheat the broiler to high and preheat the oven to 300°F. Broil the bacon for 7–8 minutes, until just starting to crisp. Drain on paper towels, slice in half widthwise, and set aside. Reserve the fat in the broiler pan.

2 Heat a skillet over medium heat, add the sausages, and cook, turning, for about 15 minutes, until evenly browned. If necessary, use a little bacon fat to prevent the sausages from sticking. Remove the sausages from the skillet, slice in half widthwise, and set aside.

3 Using the sausage skillet, gently cook the onions for 7 minutes, until soft but not browned. Add more bacon fat, if necessary.

4 Layer the onions, sausages, and bacon in the bottom of a flameproof casserole dish or Dutch oven, seasoning each layer with plenty of black pepper. Add the leek, herbs, and garlic, and finish with a layer of potatoes. Season with a little more black pepper, then pour in the broth.

5 Cover the casserole tightly and bring to a boil on top of the stove. Transfer to the preheated oven and cook for 45 minutes, or until the potatoes are tender. Serve with chunks of soda bread to mop up the juices.

CLASSIC FAVORITES

OATS & RASPBERRY CREAM

Serves: 6

Prep: 20–25 minutes, Cook: 4–5 minutes
plus cooling and chilling

Ingredients

1 cup rolled oats

1½ cups heavy cream

½ cup light cream

3 tablespoons Irish whiskey

2 tablespoons honey,
plus extra for drizzling

3 cups raspberries

Method

1 Preheat the broiler to medium. Spread out the oats on a baking sheet, place under the preheated broiler, and toast for 4–5 minutes, or until golden brown, stirring often to prevent them from burning. Transfer to a shallow bowl and let cool.

2 Combine the two creams, whiskey, and honey in a mixing bowl. Stir in the oats, mixing well. Cover with plastic wrap and let stand in the refrigerator for at least 2 hours or overnight to thicken. Stir occasionally to break up any clumps of oats.

3 Set aside about 1 cup of the best raspberries to decorate. Lightly swirl the remaining raspberries into the oat mixture, creating attractive pink streaks. Spoon into glass serving dishes and decorate with the reserved raspberries. Drizzle with honey just before serving.

CLASSIC FAVORITES

SCAILTIN (MILK PUNCH)

Serves: 2   **Prep: 15 minutes**   **Cook: 5–10 minutes**

Ingredients

2 cups milk

½ cup Irish whiskey

1–2 tablespoons honey, or to taste

⅛ teaspoon ground ginger

⅛ teaspoon ground cinnamon

freshly grated nutmeg, to decorate

Method

1 Pour the milk and whiskey into a small saucepan and stir in the honey, ginger, and cinnamon.

2 Heat slowly, without letting the mixture boil, whisking briskly all the time to create a froth and to disperse the ground spices.

3 Pour into two warm mugs and sprinkle with grated nutmeg.

CLASSIC FAVORITES

CHICKEN, MUSHROOM & TARRAGON PIE

Serves: 4–6

Prep: 35–40 minutes, plus cooling and chilling   **Cook: 2 hours 20 minutes**

Ingredients

1 chicken, about 3¼ pounds

2 fresh tarragon sprigs

1 onion, cut into wedges

1¼ cups water

2 tablespoons butter

3 cups sliced cremini mushrooms

2 tablespoons all-purpose flour

⅓ cup frozen peas or shelled fresh peas

1 tablespoon chopped fresh tarragon

salt and pepper

Pastry dough

1¾ cups all-purpose flour, plus extra for dusting

pinch of salt

1½ sticks butter

¼ cup iced water, plus extra for brushing

1 egg, beaten

Method

1 Preheat the oven to 400°F.

2 Put the chicken, tarragon sprigs, and onion into a casserole dish or Dutch oven, add the water, and season with salt and pepper to taste. Cover and bake in the preheated oven for 1½ hours. Remove from the oven and lift out the chicken from the casserole dish. Strain the cooking juices into a heatproof bowl and let cool.

3 Meanwhile, make the dough. Sift the flour with a pinch of salt into a bowl and add the butter and water. Mix to a firm but slightly lumpy dough, adding more iced water, if necessary. Roll out on a floured surface into a rectangle, then fold the top third down and the bottom third up. Give the dough a quarter turn, roll out, and fold again. Repeat once again, then wrap in plastic wrap and chill in the refrigerator.

4 Discard the chicken skin, cut off the meat, and dice. Skim off the fat from the cooking juices and make up to 1¼ cups with water.

5 Melt the butter in a large saucepan. Cook the mushrooms over medium heat for 3 minutes. Stir in the flour for 1 minute, then gradually stir in the

cooking juices. Bring to a boil, add the chicken, peas, and tarragon, and season. Transfer to a pie plate and let cool.

6   Roll out the dough to 1 inch larger than the top of the pie plate. Cut out a ⅝-inch strip all the way around. Brush the rim of the dish with water and press the strip onto it. Brush with water and lift the remaining dough on top. Trim off the excess and crimp the edges to seal. Make a slit in the center to let steam escape and brush with half of the egg. Roll out the scraps and use to decorate the pie, then brush with the remaining egg. Bake in the preheated oven for 40 minutes, until golden brown. Serve immediately.

COLCANNON

Serves: 4   **Prep: 25 minutes**   **Cook: 25–30 minutes**

Ingredients

2⅓ cups shredded green cabbage

⅓ cup milk

2 russet potatoes, diced

1 large leek, chopped

pinch of freshly grated nutmeg

pat of butter

salt and pepper

Method

1 Cook the shredded cabbage in a saucepan of boiling salted water for 7–10 minutes. Drain thoroughly and set aside.

2 Meanwhile, in a separate saucepan, bring the milk to a boil and add the potatoes and leek. Reduce the heat and simmer for 15–20 minutes, or until they are cooked through. Remove from the heat, stir in the freshly grated nutmeg, and thoroughly mash together the potatoes and leek.

3 Add the drained cabbage to the mashed potato-and-leek mixture, season to taste with salt and pepper, and mix together well.

4 Spoon the mixture into a warm serving dish, making a hollow in the center with the back of a spoon. Place the butter on top and serve the colcannon at once, while it is still hot.

HAM STEAK WITH EGGS & FRIES

Serves: 4   **Prep: 30 minutes**   **Cook: 30–35 minutes**

Ingredients

vegetable oil, for frying and brushing

6 russet potatoes (about 1½ pounds), cut into even sticks

4 cured ham steaks (about 6 ounces each)

4 eggs

salt and pepper

Method

1 To blanch the potatoes, heat enough oil for deep-frying in a large saucepan or deep fryer to 250°F (check with a thermometer). Preheat the oven to 300°F.

2 Cook the potatoes for 8–10 minutes, depending on their size, until soft but not browned. Remove from the oil, drain on paper towels, and place in a warm dish in the preheated oven. Increase the temperature of the oil to 350–375°F, or until a cube of bread browns in 30 seconds.

3 Meanwhile, put the ham steaks on a broiler pan and brush with a little oil. Preheat the broiler to high and broil for 3–4 minutes on each side, turning occasionally, until the fat is crisp. Set aside and keep warm.

4 Return the potatoes to the fryer at the increased temperature and cook for 2–3 minutes, until they are golden brown and crisp. Drain, season well, and keep warm. Put 2 tablespoons of oil into a skillet and heat over medium heat. Break two eggs into the pan and cook for a few seconds, until the white is setting. Tilt the pan and spoon the hot oil over the egg yolks so that they become firm but remain soft. Remove the eggs from the pan, using a spatula, and drain on paper towels. Keep warm and repeat with the other eggs.

5 Arrange the ham steaks, egg, and fries on warm plates and serve immediately.

CLASSIC FAVORITES

PORK CHOPS WITH APPLE SAUCE

Serves: 4   **Prep: 20–25 minutes**   **Cook: 30 minutes, plus standing**

Ingredients

4 pork rib chops on the bone (each about 1¼ inches thick), at room temperature

1½ tablespoons sunflower oil or canola oil

salt and pepper

Chunky applesauce

3 cooking apples, such as Granny Smith, peeled, cored, and diced

¼ cup sugar, plus extra if needed

finely grated zest of ½ lemon

1½ teaspoons lemon juice, plus extra if needed

¼ cup water

¼ teaspoon ground cinnamon

pat of butter

Method

1 Preheat the oven to 400°F.

2 For the applesauce, put the apples, sugar, lemon zest, lemon juice, and water into a heavy saucepan over high heat and bring to a boil, stirring, to dissolve the sugar. Reduce the heat to low, cover, and simmer for 15–20 minutes, until the apples are tender and fall apart when you mash them against the side of the pan. Stir in the cinnamon and butter and beat the apples until they are as smooth or chunky as you prefer. Stir in extra sugar or lemon juice to taste. Remove the pan from the heat, cover, and keep the applesauce warm.

3 Meanwhile, pat the chops dry and season to taste with salt and pepper. Heat the oil in a large ovenproof skillet over medium–high heat. Add the chops and cook for 3 minutes on each side to brown.

4 Transfer the pan to the oven and roast the chops for 7–9 minutes, until cooked through and the juices run clear when you cut into the chops. Remove the pan from the oven, cover with aluminum foil, and let stand for 3 minutes. Gently reheat the applesauce, if needed. Transfer the chops to warm plates and spoon the pan juices over them. Serve immediately with the applesauce.

CLASSIC FAVORITES

APPLE PIE

Serves: 6

Prep: 40–45 minutes, Cook: 50 minutes
plus chilling

Ingredients

Pastry dough

2¾ cups all-purpose flour,
plus extra for dusting

pinch of salt

6 tablespoons butter or
margarine, diced

⅓ cup lard or vegetable
shortening, diced

⅓ cup cold water

beaten egg or milk,
for glazing

Filling

5–6 cooking apples,
such as Granny Smith
(about 1¾–2¼ pounds),
peeled, cored, and sliced

⅔ cup granulated sugar,
plus extra for sprinkling

½–1 teaspoon ground
cinnamon, allspice,
or ground ginger

Method

1 To make the dough, sift the flour and salt into a
mixing bowl. Add the butter and lard and rub in
with your fingertips until the mixture resembles fine
bread crumbs. Add the water and gather the
mixture together into a dough. Wrap the dough
in plastic wrap and chill in the refrigerator for
30 minutes.

2 Preheat the oven to 425°F. Roll out almost two-thirds
of the dough thinly on a lightly floured surface and
use to line a deep 9-inch pie plate.

3 To make the filling, put the apple slices, sugar, and
spice into a bowl and mix together thoroughly. Pack
the apple mixture into the pastry shell; the filling can
come up above the rim. If the apples are not juicy,
add 1–2 tablespoons of water, if needed.

4 Roll out the remaining dough on a lightly floured
surface to form a lid. Dampen the edges of the
pie rim with water and position the lid, pressing the
edges firmly together. Trim the edges. Use the scraps
to cut out leaves to decorate the top of the pie.
Dampen and attach. Glaze the top of the pie with
beaten egg, make one or two slits in the top, and
place the pie plate on a baking sheet.

5 Bake in the preheated oven for 20 minutes, then
reduce the temperature to 350°F and bake for an
additional 30 minutes, or until the pastry is a light
golden brown. Serve hot or cold.

CLASSIC FAVORITES

FISHERMAN'S PIE

Serves: 6 **Prep: 35–40 minutes** **Cook: 1 hour**

Ingredients

2 pounds white fish fillets, such as flounder or halibut, skinned

⅔ cup white wine

1 tablespoon chopped fresh parsley, tarragon or dill

1 stick butter, plus extra for greasing

3 cups sliced white button mushrooms

6 ounces cooked, peeled shrimp

⅓ cup all-purpose flour

½ cup heavy cream

8 russet potatoes (about 2 pounds), cut into chunks

salt and pepper

Method

1 Preheat the oven to 350°F. Grease a 1¾-quart baking dish. Fold the fish fillets in half, if thin, and put into the dish. Season well with salt and pepper, pour the wine over the fish, and sprinkle with the herbs. Cover with aluminum foil and bake for 15 minutes, until the fish starts to flake. Strain off the liquid and reserve for the sauce. Increase the oven temperature to 425°F.

2 Heat 1 tablespoon of the butter in a skillet and sauté the mushrooms. Spoon the mushrooms over the fish and sprinkle with the shrimp. Add 4 tablespoons of the butter to a saucepan, heat, and stir in the flour. Cook for a few minutes without browning, remove from the heat, then add the reserved cooking liquid gradually, stirring well between each addition.

3 Return to the heat and gently bring to a boil, still stirring to be sure of a smooth sauce. Add the cream and season to taste with salt and pepper. Pour it over the fish in the dish and smooth over the surface.

4 Make the mashed potatoes by cooking the potatoes in boiling salted water for 15–20 minutes. Drain well and mash with a potato masher until smooth. Season to taste with salt and pepper and add the remaining butter.

5 Pile or pipe the potato onto the fish and sauce and bake in the oven for 10–15 minutes, until golden brown.

CLASSIC FAVORITES

VEGETABLE COBBLER

Serves: 4   **Prep: 35–40 minutes   Cook: 40 minutes**

Ingredients

1 tablespoon olive oil

1 garlic clove, crushed

8 small onions, halved

2 celery stalks, sliced

1⅔ cups chopped rutabaga

2 carrots, sliced

½ small head of cauliflower, broken into florets

3 cups sliced white mushrooms

1 (14-ounce) can diced tomatoes

¼ cup red lentils, rinsed

2 tablespoons cornstarch

3–4 tablespoons water

1¼ cups vegetable broth

2 teaspoons Tabasco sauce

2 teaspoons chopped fresh oregano, plus sprigs to garnish

Topping

1¾ cups all-purpose flour, plus extra for dusting

1¾ teaspoons baking powder

pinch of salt

4 tablespoons butter

1 cup shredded sharp cheddar cheese

2 teaspoons chopped fresh oregano

1 egg, lightly beaten

⅔ cup milk

Method

1 Preheat the oven to 350°F. Heat the oil in a large skillet, add the garlic and onions, and sauté over low heat for 5 minutes. Add the celery, rutabaga, carrots, and cauliflower and cook for 2–3 minutes.

2 Add the mushrooms, tomatoes, and lentils. Put the cornstarch and water into a bowl and mix to make a smooth paste. Stir into the skillet with the broth, Tabasco sauce, and oregano. Transfer to an ovenproof dish, cover, and bake in the preheated oven for 20 minutes.

3 To make the topping, sift together the flour, baking powder, and salt into a bowl. Add the butter and rub it in, then stir in most of the cheese and oregano. Beat the egg with the milk in a small bowl and add enough to the dry ingredients to make a soft dough. Knead, then roll out on a lightly floured work surface to ½ inch thick. Cut into 2-inch circles.

4 Remove the dish from the oven and increase the temperature to 400°F. Arrange the dough circles around the edge of the dish, brush with the remaining egg-and-milk mixture, and sprinkle with the reserved cheese. Return to the oven and cook for an additional 10–12 minutes. Garnish with oregano sprigs and serve.

CLASSIC FAVORITES

MERINGUE WITH STRAWBERRIES

Serves: 6

Prep: 30–35 minutes, Cook: 45–50 minutes
plus cooling

Ingredients

3 egg whites

¾ cup plus 2 tablespoons superfine sugar

1½ pounds strawberries

2 tablespoons confectioners' sugar

2 tablespoons crème de fraise (strawberry) liqueur (optional)

1¼ cups heavy cream

⅔ cup light cream

Method

1 Preheat the oven to 300°F. Whisk the egg whites in a clean bowl, using an electric mixer, until thick and in soft peaks. Add the sugar gradually, whisking well after each addition. The meringue mixture should be glossy and firm. Spoon the meringue onto a baking sheet lined with parchment paper and spread into an approximate 12-inch circle. Cook in the preheated oven for 45–50 minutes, until the meringue is firm on the outside but still soft in the center. Remove from the oven and let cool.

2 Check over the strawberries and hull them. Put one-third of the strawberries (choose the larger ones) into a liquidizer and puree with the confectioners' sugar. Pour the puree into a bowl, add the liqueur, if using, and the remaining strawberries, and turn in the sauce until well mixed. Whip together the heavy cream and light cream until thick but still light and floppy.

3 Break the meringue into large pieces and put half into a large glass serving bowl. Spoon half the fruit mixture and half the cream over the top. Layer up the remaining ingredients and lightly fold the mixtures together so you have a streaky appearance. Serve immediately after mixing or the meringues will soften.

CLASSIC FAVORITES

RICE PUDDING WITH POACHED RHUBARB

Serves: 12

Prep: 25 minutes, plus cooling

Cook: 1½ hours

Ingredients

butter, for greasing

5½ cups whole milk or low-fat milk

½ cup short-grain rice

¼ cup granulated sugar

1 teaspoon vanilla extract

freshly grated nutmeg, for sprinkling

Poached rhubarb

8 rhubarb stalks, cut into 2-inch pieces (about 3 cups)

½ cup granulated sugar

3 tablespoons water

1–2 tablespoons rose water or rose syrup

Method

1 Preheat the oven to 325°F. Grease a 1½-quart baking dish. Put the milk into a large, heavy saucepan and bring to a boil. Add the rice and boil for 10 minutes, stirring constantly at first, so that it doesn't boil over.

2 Remove from the heat, then stir in the sugar and vanilla extract. Transfer to the prepared dish and sprinkle with nutmeg. Bake in the preheated oven for 1¼ hours, or until a brown skin has formed on top and the pudding is still wobbly underneath.

3 Meanwhile, put the rhubarb into a baking dish or roasting pan just large enough to hold the pieces in a single layer. Add the sugar and water, and then stir the mixture.

4 Cover the dish tightly with aluminum foil and bake in the preheated oven for 30 minutes, or until the rhubarb is just tender when pierced with the point of a knife (thick stems may need a little longer). Cool for at least 15 minutes, keeping the foil in place, then gently stir in the rose water to taste. Spoon the rhubarb over the rice pudding and serve.

CLASSIC FAVORITES

HOMEMADE FISH STICKS

Serves: 8　　　　**Prep: 25 minutes**　　　　**Cook: 50–60 minutes**

Ingredients

10 ounces thick cod fillets, skin and bones removed

flour, for dusting

1 teaspoon paprika

fresh bread crumbs or fine cornmeal, for coating

1 egg, beaten

sunflower oil, for frying

salt and pepper

fresh or frozen peas, cooked, to serve

Sweet potato wedges

2–3 sweet potatoes (about 1 pound), scrubbed and cut into wedges

1 tablespoon olive oil

Method

1 To make the potato wedges, preheat the oven to 400°F. Dry the sweet potato wedges on a clean dish towel. Put the oil into a roasting pan and heat for a few minutes in the oven. Arrange the potatoes in the pan and bake for 30–35 minutes, turning them halfway through, until tender and golden.

2 Meanwhile, cut the cod into strips about ¾-inch wide. Put the flour onto a plate, add the paprika, and season to taste. Put the bread crumbs onto a second plate. Roll the cod strips in the seasoned flour until coated, shaking off any excess, then dip them in the beaten egg. Roll the cod strips in the bread crumbs until evenly coated.

3 Heat enough oil to cover the bottom of a large, nonstick skillet. Carefully arrange the fish strips in the pan—you may have to cook them in batches—and cook them for 3–4 minutes on each side or until crisp and golden. Drain on paper towels before serving, if necessary. Serve the fish sticks with the sweet potato wedges and peas.

WINTER VEGETABLE SOUP

Serves: 6   **Prep: 20 minutes**   **Cook: 50 minutes**

Ingredients

2 tablespoons vegetable oil

1 large onion, thickly sliced

1 large Yukon gold or red-skinned potato, cut into chunks

3 celery stalks, thickly sliced

4 carrots, sliced

1 cup rutabaga chunks

4 large garlic cloves, peeled and left whole

6⅓ cups chicken or vegetable broth

1 cup canned diced tomatoes

1 leek, halved lengthwise and thickly sliced

salt and pepper

2 tablespoons chopped fresh flat-leaf parsley, to garnish

shredded cheddar cheese, to serve

Method

1 Heat the oil in a large, heavy saucepan over medium heat. Add the onion, potato, celery, carrots, rutabaga, and garlic cloves. Season to taste with salt and pepper, then cover and cook over medium heat, stirring occasionally, for 10 minutes.

2 Pour in the broth and tomatoes and bring to a boil. Reduce the heat and simmer, partly covered, for 30 minutes. Add the leek and cook for an additional 5 minutes, until just tender.

3 Taste and adjust the seasoning, adding salt and pepper, if needed. Ladle into warm bowls, garnish with the parsley, and serve immediately with shredded cheddar cheese.

SUMMER ROASTED CHICKEN

Serves: 4

Prep: 30 minutes

Cook: 1 hour 35 minutes, plus resting

Ingredients

1¼ pounds new potatoes, scrubbed and larger ones halved

1 chicken (about 3¼ pounds)

1 lemon (preferably unwaxed)

1 tablespoon chopped fresh thyme

2 tablespoons olive oil

3 bay leaves

1 garlic bulb, cloves separated

salt and pepper

green salad, to serve

Method

1 Parboil the potatoes in a saucepan of lightly salted boiling water for 10 minutes, then drain. Preheat the oven to 375°F.

2 Loosen the skin over the chicken breast by pushing your fingers underneath, being careful not to tear it. Pare the zest from the lemon and mix it with the thyme, then push the mixture underneath the skin of the chicken. Drizzle in 2 teaspoons of the oil and season with salt and pepper. Cut the lemon in half and push the two pieces inside the body cavity with the bay leaves, then truss the chicken.

3 Transfer the potatoes to a large roasting pan. Add the garlic and remainder of the olive oil and toss together. Make a space for the chicken in the center of the roasting pan and roast in the preheated oven for 1 hour 25 minutes, stirring and turning the potatoes once or twice during cooking. To check the chicken is cooked through, pierce the thickest part of the thigh with the tip of a sharp knife—when the juices run clear, it is ready. Cover and rest the chicken for 10–15 minutes before carving. Serve with the roasted new potatoes and green salad.

CARAMELIZED ONION TART

Serves: 4-6

Prep: 25 minutes, plus resting

Cook: 50–55 minutes

Ingredients

1 stick unsalted butter

3 onions, thinly sliced

2 eggs

½ cup heavy cream

1 cup shredded Gruyère or Swiss cheese

1 (8–9-inch) baked piecrust

1 cup coarsely grated Parmesan cheese

salt and pepper

Method

1 Melt the butter in a heavy skillet over medium heat. Add the onions and cook, stirring frequently to prevent them from burning, for 30 minutes, or until well browned and caramelized. Remove the onions from the pan and set aside.

2 Preheat the oven to 375°F. Beat the eggs in a large bowl. Stir in the cream and season to taste with salt and pepper. Add the Gruyère cheese and mix well. Stir in the cooked onions.

3 Pour the egg-and-onion mixture into the baked piecrust and sprinkle with the Parmesan cheese.

4 Place on a baking sheet and bake in the preheated oven for 15–20 minutes, until the filling has set and is beginning to brown. Remove from the oven and let rest for at least 10 minutes.

5 Cut the tart into slices and serve hot or at room temperature.

★ **Variation**

For a delicious accompanying salad, wash some arugula, cherry tomatoes, and add ¼ cup of parmesan cheese and 2 tablespoons of olive oil. Mix together and season to taste.

HOME COMFORTS

LUXURY CAULIFLOWER & CHEESE

Serves: 4   **Prep: 25 minutes**   **Cook: 30–40 minutes**

Ingredients

1 head of cauliflower, trimmed and cut into florets

⅔ cup dry white wine

1 bay leaf

2 cups milk

2 tablespoons butter, cut into pieces

3 tablespoons all-purpose flour

½ cup shredded sharp cheddar cheese

½ cup grated Parmesan cheese

1 teaspoon English mustard

1 tablespoon snipped fresh chives

1 tablespoon chopped fresh parsley

salt

Method

1 Cook the cauliflower in a large saucepan of lightly salted boiling water for 6–8 minutes, until tender but still firm to the bite. Drain well. Preheat the oven to 400°F. Alternatively, preheat the broiler to high.

2 Put the wine and bay leaf into a saucepan. Boil rapidly until the wine is reduced by half. Add the milk, butter, and flour and whisk with a wire whisk until the butter has melted. Continue whisking until the sauce boils and thickens. Simmer for 1 minute.

3 Remove from the heat. Mix the cheeses together and stir two-thirds into the sauce until smooth, then stir in the mustard, chives, and parsley. Remove the bay leaf from the sauce and discard.

4 Spoon a little of the sauce over the bottom of a shallow baking dish. Add the cauliflower to the dish and spread it out in an even layer. Spoon the remaining sauce over the top and then sprinkle with the rest of the cheese. Bake in the preheated oven for 20 minutes, until lightly browned and bubbling. Alternatively, brown the dish under the broiler. Serve hot.

★ Variation

For an extra delicious dish, dice some cooked bacon or cut into strips and sprinkle over the top.

LEEK & POTATO SOUP

Serves: 4-6　　　　**Prep: 20-25 minutes**　　**Cook: 30 minutes**

Ingredients

4 tablespoons butter

1 onion, chopped

3 leeks, sliced

2 Yukon gold or red-skinned potatoes, cut into ¾-inch cubes

3½ cups vegetable broth

salt and pepper

⅔ cup light cream (optional), to serve

2 tablespoons snipped fresh chives, to garnish

Method

1 Melt the butter in a large saucepan over medium heat, add the prepared vegetables, and sauté gently for 2–3 minutes, until soft but not brown. Pour in the broth and bring to a boil, then reduce the heat and simmer, covered, for 15 minutes.

2 Remove from the heat and puree the soup in the saucepan, using a handheld immersion blender, if you have one. Alternatively, pour into a blender, puree until smooth, and return to the rinsed-out saucepan.

3 Reheat the soup and season to taste with salt and pepper. Ladle into warm bowls and serve, swirled with the cream, if using, and garnished with the chives.

CREAM OF TOMATO SOUP

Serves: 6   **Prep: 25 minutes**   **Cook: 30–40 minutes**

Ingredients

2 tablespoons butter

1 tablespoon olive oil

1 onion, finely chopped

1 garlic clove, chopped

14–15 plum tomatoes
(about 2 pounds), chopped

3 cups vegetable broth

½ cup dry white wine

2 tablespoons
tomato paste

2 tablespoons torn fresh
basil leaves, plus extra
leaves to garnish

⅔ cup heavy cream

salt and pepper

Method

1 Melt the butter with the oil in a large, heavy saucepan. Add the onion and sauté, stirring occasionally, for 5 minutes, or until softened. Add the garlic, tomatoes, broth, wine, and tomato paste, stir well, and season to taste. Partly cover the saucepan and simmer, stirring occasionally, for 20–25 minutes, or until the mixture is soft and pulpy.

2 Remove the saucepan from the heat, let cool slightly, then pour into a blender or food processor. Add the torn basil and process. Push the mixture through a strainer into a clean saucepan with a wooden spoon.

3 Stir in the cream and reheat the soup, but do not let it boil. Ladle the soup into warm bowls, garnish with the basil leaves, and serve immediately.

QUICHE LORRAINE

Serves: 4

Prep: 30–35 minutes,   Cook: 50 minutes
plus cooling

Ingredients

4 eggs

6 ounces cooked ham

3 scallions,
finely chopped

⅔ cup milk, plus extra
to glaze

salt and pepper

Pastry dough

2 cups all-purpose flour

1 stick butter

pinch of salt

2–3 tablespoons cold water,
to mix

Method

1 Preheat the oven to 400°F.

2 To make the dough, put the flour into a bowl, rub in the butter until the mixture resembles fine bread crumbs, then add the salt and enough water to make a smooth dough.

3 Bring a saucepan of water to a boil. Gently lower two of the eggs into the water using a long-handle spoon. Keep the water at a gentle simmer and cook for 8 minutes. Remove the eggs and cool under cold running water.

4 Divide the dough in two, one piece slightly larger than the other, and roll out the larger piece to line an 8-inch tart pan.

5 Peel the hard-boiled eggs carefully and wipe to make sure there are no pieces of shell attached to the eggs. Chop the eggs and cut the ham into small pieces. Put the eggs, ham, and onions into the pastry shell.

6 Beat the remaining eggs with the milk, season well with salt and pepper, and pour the mixture over the ham and eggs.

7 Roll out the other piece of dough, dampen the edge of the pastry shell, and lay the lid on top. Seal well and crimp the edges of the quiche. Glaze with a little milk and place the quiche on a baking sheet.

8 Bake in the preheated oven for 10 minutes, then reduce the oven temperature to 350°F and bake for an additional 30 minutes, until the pastry is golden. Serve warm or cold.

TANGY MELTED CHEESE ON TOAST

Serves: 4   **Prep: 20 minutes**   **Cook: 5 minutes**

Ingredients

2 cups shredded mild cheddar cheese

2 tablespoons salted butter

¼ cup milk

1 teaspoon apple cider vinegar

1 teaspoon dry mustard

4 slices whole wheat or soda bread

2 tablespoons chopped dill pickles

salt and pepper

Method

1 Preheat the broiler until hot. Put the cheese, butter, and milk into a saucepan and heat gently, stirring, until creamy and smooth. Add the vinegar, mustard, and seasoning to the sauce.

2 Toast the bread on only one side. Place on a baking sheet, untoasted side facing upward. Pour the sauce over the bread. Put under the preheated broiler for 2–3 minutes, until golden and bubbling.

3 Sprinkle with the chopped pickles and serve immediately.

BAKED EGGS WITH CREAM, SPINACH & PARMESAN

Serves: 2   **Prep: 20 minutes**   **Cook: 12 minutes**

Ingredients

2 tablespoons butter, plus extra for greasing

4½ cups baby spinach

½ teaspoon freshly grated nutmeg

4 medium eggs

¼ cup light cream

2 tablespoons freshly grated Parmesan cheese

salt and pepper

Method

1 Preheat the oven to 325°F. Lightly grease two individual ceramic gratin dishes, or similar.

2 Melt the butter in a large skillet over low heat and add the spinach. Cook for 1 minute, stirring with a wooden spoon, until the spinach starts to wilt. Season with a little nutmeg, then divide between the prepared dishes.

3 Gently break two eggs into each dish. Pour the cream over them and sprinkle with grated Parmesan, then season with salt and pepper. Bake in the preheated oven for 10 minutes, or until the whites of the eggs have set but the yolks remain runny. Serve immediately.

BACON & POTATO CAKES

Serves: 4 **Prep: 30 minutes** **Cook: 35–40 minutes**

Ingredients

4 russet potatoes, cut into even chunks

8 thin bacon strips

1 tablespoon salted butter

½ teaspoon sea salt flakes

½ teaspoon pepper

2 tablespoons snipped chives

¼ cup rolled oats

1 egg, lightly beaten

all-purpose flour, for dusting

canola oil or vegetable oil, for frying

peppery greens, to garnish (optional)

Method

1 Put the potatoes into a large saucepan of salted boiling water, cover, bring back to a boil, and simmer gently for 20 minutes, until tender. Drain well and put back into the pan. Cover with a clean dish cloth for a few minutes to get rid of any excess moisture.

2 While the potatoes are cooking, cook the bacon over medium–high heat for 5–6 minutes, until crisp. Drain on paper towels. Set aside four strips and keep warm. Finely chop the remaining strips.

3 Mash the potatoes with the butter, sea salt, and pepper until creamy. Stir in the chopped bacon, chives, oats, and beaten egg.

4 With floured hands, form the potato mixture into four flat cakes about 2¾ inches in diameter.

5 Heat about ½ inch of oil in a heavy saucepan over medium heat. Add the potato cakes and cook for about 4 minutes on each side, until golden brown.

6 Transfer the potato cakes to warm serving plates. Top with the peppery greens, if using, and reserved bacon strips, and serve immediately.

HOME COMFORTS

BEEF & STOUT PIES

Serves: 4

Prep: 35–40 minutes, plus cooling

Cook: 2 hours 20 minutes

Ingredients

3 tablespoons all-purpose flour

1 teaspoon salt, plus extra to taste

½ teaspoon pepper, plus extra to taste

2 pounds boneless beef chuck, cut into 1-inch pieces

vegetable oil, for frying

1¼ cups beef broth

1 onion, coarsely chopped

8 ounces cremini mushrooms, stems discarded, caps quartered

1 tablespoon tomato paste

2 teaspoons chopped fresh thyme

1 cup stout

1 (1-pound) package ready-to-bake puff pastry, thawed if frozen

1 egg yolk, lightly beaten

Method

1 Combine the flour, salt, and pepper in a bowl, then toss the beef in the mixture until evenly coated.

2 Heat 3 tablespoons of oil in a large skillet over medium–high heat. Brown the beef, in batches, and transfer to a flameproof casserole dish or Dutch oven. Deglaze the skillet with ¼ cup of the broth and add the liquid to the casserole.

3 Heat another 1–2 tablespoons of oil in the skillet and sauté the onion and mushrooms for 6–7 minutes, until soft. Add to the casserole with the tomato paste, thyme, stout, and remaining broth. Heat the casserole over medium–high heat, bring to a boil, then simmer gently with the lid slightly askew for 1½ hours. Check the seasoning and adjust, if necessary.

4 Drain the meat mixture in a strainer set over a bowl, reserving the liquid. Let stand until cool. Preheat the oven to 425°F. Put a baking sheet in the oven to heat.

5 Divide the meat mixture among four individual 1¾-cup pie plates with a flat rim or ovenproof bowls. Pour in enough of the liquid to almost cover the filling. Dampen the rims of the pie plates.

6 Cut the pastry into quarters. Roll out each piece to about 1 inch bigger than the dishes. Cut a ½-inch strip from each quarter and press it onto a dampened rim. Brush with egg yolk, then drape the pastry quarter on top, covering the strip. Trim, crimp the edges with a fork, and make three slashes down the middle. Decorate the tops with shapes cut from the scraps. Brush with the remaining egg yolk.

7 Place the pies on the preheated baking sheet and bake in the preheated oven for 20 minutes. Reduce the heat to 400°F and bake for an additional 5 minutes, until golden.

YAM, TURNIP & MUSHROOM HASH

Serves: 4   **Prep: 20–25 minutes**   **Cook: 25–30 minutes**

Ingredients

3 tablespoons olive oil

3 cups diced yams or sweet potatoes

2 cups diced turnips

1 onion, chopped

6 ounces bacon, sliced or diced

3 cups sliced white button mushrooms

4 eggs

salt and pepper

chopped fresh parsley, to garnish

Method

1 Heat the oil in a large, lidded skillet over high heat. Add the yams and turnips, stir in the oil to coat, and season to taste with salt and pepper. Cook, stirring occasionally, for 10–15 minutes, or until the vegetables are just turning golden and soft.

2 Add the onion and bacon, stir well, and continue to cook for 5 minutes, until the onion is soft and the bacon is cooked. Stir in the mushrooms, cover the pan, and cook for an additional 5 minutes.

3 Make four indentations in the mixture and carefully break an egg into each one. Cover the pan and cook for an additional 3–4 minutes, or until the egg whites are firm but the yolks are still soft. Garnish with parsley and serve immediately.

HAM STEAKS WITH PARSLEY SAUCE

Serves: 4　　　　**Prep: 20 minutes**　　　　**Cook: 30–40 minutes**

Ingredients

4 unsmoked cured ham steaks (about 7 ounces each and ¾ inch thick)

vegetable oil, for brushing

Parsley sauce

2 tablespoons unsalted butter

1 shallot, finely chopped

3 tablespoons all-purpose flour

¾ cup chicken broth

1 cup milk

⅓ cup chopped fresh parsley

squeeze of lemon juice

½ teaspoon dry mustard

salt and white pepper

Method

1 First, make the parsley sauce. Melt the butter in a skillet over medium–low heat. Add the shallot and cook for 2–3 minutes, until soft but not browned.

2 Remove the skillet from the heat and stir in the flour. Return to the heat and cook for 1 minute, stirring. Reduce the heat to low and whisk in the broth and milk. Keep whisking until the sauce starts to simmer. Stir in the parsley, then add the lemon juice, mustard, pepper, and a pinch of salt. Simmer gently, stirring often, for 20 minutes.

3 Meanwhile, remove the rind but not the fat from the ham steaks. Slash the fat at ¾-inch intervals. Brush with oil on both sides.

4 Heat a ridged grill pan over high heat. Cook the steaks on one side for 5–6 minutes. Once they start to brown on the underside, cover with a lid and reduce the heat to medium. Turn and cook the other side for 5 minutes, covered.

5 Put the steaks onto warm serving plates, pour the sauce over them, and serve.

QUICK SPAGHETTI BOLOGNESE

Serves: 4   **Prep: 20 minutes**   **Cook: 35 minutes**

Ingredients

2 tablespoons olive oil

1 large onion, chopped

1 pound ground round beef

1 green bell pepper, seeded and chopped

1 garlic clove, crushed

⅔ cup red wine or beef broth

1 (14-ounce) can diced plum tomatoes

2 tablespoons tomato paste

1 tablespoon dried oregano

8 ounces dried spaghetti

salt and pepper

freshly grated Parmesan cheese, to serve

Method

1 Heat the oil in a large saucepan over high heat.

2 Add the onion and beef and sauté, stirring, until lightly browned with no remaining traces of pink.

3 Stir in the green bell pepper and garlic. Add the wine, tomatoes, tomato paste, and oregano. Bring to a boil and boil rapidly for 2 minutes.

4 Reduce the heat, cover, and simmer for 20 minutes, stirring occasionally.

5 Meanwhile, bring a large saucepan of lightly salted water to a boil, add the spaghetti, bring back to a boil, and cook for 8–10 minutes, or according to the package directions, until tender but still firm to the bite.

6 Drain the spaghetti in a colander and return to the pan.

7 Season the meat sauce to taste with salt and pepper, then stir into the spaghetti.

8 Serve immediately, with Parmesan cheese.

SAUSAGE ROLLS

Makes: 8

Prep: 25–30 minutes,   Cook: 30–35 minutes
plus cooling

Ingredients

2 teaspoons sunflower oil

1 small onion,
finely chopped

2 teaspoons chopped fresh
sage

1 pound pork sausagemeat
(or sausage links with
casings removed)

2 teaspoons
whole-grain mustard

½ cup fresh white
bread crumbs

1 sheet ready-to-bake
puff pastry, thawed if frozen

salt and pepper

1 egg beaten
with 1 tablespoon water,
to glaze

Method

1 Heat the oil in a skillet and gently sauté the chopped onion for 8–10 minutes, until soft and pale golden. Transfer to a large bowl, stir in the chopped sage, and let cool. Preheat the oven to 400°F.

2 Add the sausagemeat to the bowl with the mustard and bread crumbs. Season with salt and pepper and mix thoroughly with a fork. Unroll the pastry sheet and cut in half lengthwise. Divide the sausage meat mixture into two equal portions and lay along the length of each strip of pastry, forming into a cylinder shape.

3 Brush one long edge of each strip of pastry with some of the egg-and-water mixture and fold over the pastry to enclose the filling. Press the edges together well to seal and cut each roll into four shorter lengths. Lightly dampen a large baking sheet with cold water and place the sausage rolls on it, spaced well apart. Glaze the pastry with the egg-and-water mixture. Bake in the preheated oven for 20–25 minutes, until crisp and golden. Transfer to a wire rack and serve warm or cold.

HOME COMFORTS

POTATO PANCAKES

Serves: 6   **Prep: 25 minutes**   **Cook: 11–17 minutes**

Ingredients

4 large russet potatoes, shredded

1 large onion, grated

2 eggs, lightly beaten

½ cup fine matzo meal

1 teaspoon salt

pepper

sunflower oil, for frying

To serve

sour cream

thinly sliced smoked salmon

snipped chives

Method

1 Preheat the oven to 25°F and line a heatproof plate with paper towels. Working in small batches, put the potatoes on a dish towel, fold over the dish towel, and squeeze to extract as much water as possible.

2 Put the potatoes into a large bowl, then add the onion, eggs, matzo meal, and salt. Add pepper to taste and mix together.

3 Heat a large, heavy skillet over medium-high heat. Add a thin layer of oil and heat until hot. Drop 2 tablespoons of the batter into the pan and flatten slightly. Add as many pancakes as will fit without overcrowding the pan. Cook for 2 minutes, or until crisp and golden underneath. Flip or turn with a spatula and continue cooking for 1–2 minutes, until crisp and golden.

4 Repeat, using the remaining batter. Meanwhile, transfer the cooked pancakes to the prepared plate and keep warm in the oven. Add extra oil to the pan between batches, if necessary. Serve the pancakes hot, topped with sour cream and salmon and sprinkled with chives.

SPAGHETTI ALLA CARBONARA

Serves: 4   **Prep: 20 minutes**   **Cook: 15 minutes**

Ingredients

1 pound dried spaghetti

1 tablespoon olive oil

8 ounces rindless pancetta or bacon, chopped

4 eggs

⅓ cup light cream

2 tablespoons freshly grated Parmesan cheese

salt and pepper

Method

1 Bring a large, heavy saucepan of lightly salted water to a boil, add the pasta, bring back to a boil, and cook for 8–10 minutes, or according to package directions, until tender but still firm to the bite.

2 Meanwhile, heat the oil in a heavy skillet. Add the pancetta and cook over medium heat, stirring frequently, for 8–10 minutes.

3 Beat the eggs with the cream in a small bowl and season to taste with salt and pepper. Drain the pasta and return to the saucepan. Add the contents of the skillet, then add the egg mixture and half the cheese. Stir well, then transfer the spaghetti to a warm serving dish. Serve immediately, sprinkled with the remaining cheese.

HOME COMFORTS

HERRING & POTATO SALAD WITH MUSTARD DRESSING

Serves: 4–6   **Prep: 25–30 minutes**   **Cook: 15–20 minutes**

Ingredients

1½ pounds new potatoes, scrubbed

3 tablespoons chopped fresh dill, plus sprigs to garnish

scallions, some green tops included, diagonally sliced

radishes, sliced into circles

10 ounces smoked herring fillets

salt and pepper

Mustard dressing

1 teaspoon dry mustard

pinch of sugar

2 tablespoons apple cider vinegar

tablespoons heavy cream

3 tablespoons peanut oil

3 tablespoons olive oil

salt and pepper

Method

1 Cook the potatoes in boiling salted water for 15–20 minutes, or until just tender. Drain and slice widthwise into ¼-inch pieces. Set aside to cool.

2 To make the dressing, combine the mustard, sugar, salt and pepper, cider vinegar, and heavy cream. Gradually add the oils, whisking until smooth and thick.

3 Put the potatoes into a bowl, then mix with the dressing and dill. Add most of the scallions and radishes, reserving a few to garnish. Check the seasoning, and add more salt and pepper, if necessary.

4 Remove the skin from the herring fillets. If large, slice each lengthwise and then widthwise into thin bite-size strips.

5 Divide the potato mixture among individual serving plates. Arrange the herring strips attractively on top, and garnish with the reserved scallions, radishes, and dill sprigs.

BACON SANDWICHES WITH HOMEMADE TOMATO SAUCE

Serves: 2

Prep: 25–30 minutes, Cook: 35 minutes
plus cooling and storing

Ingredients

Tomato sauce
(makes about 1 cup)

2 tablespoons olive oil

1 red onion, chopped

2 garlic cloves, chopped

4 plum tomatoes, chopped

2 cup canned diced tomatoes

½ teaspoon ground ginger

½ teaspoon chili powder

¼ cup firmly packed dark brown sugar

½ cup red wine vinegar

salt and pepper

Sandwich

4 smoked bacon strips

2 tablespoons butter, softened

4 slices thick white or whole wheat bread

pepper

Method

1 To make the tomato sauce, heat the olive oil in a large saucepan and add the onion, garlic, and tomatoes. Add the ginger and chili powder and season with salt and pepper to taste. Cook for 15 minutes, or until soft.

2 Pour the mixture into a food processor and blend well. Strain thoroughly to remove all the seeds. Return the mixture to the pan and add the sugar and vinegar. Return to a boil and cook until it is the consistency of ketchup.

3 Transfer quickly into a sterilized air-tight jar and store in the refrigerator until ready to serve.

4 To make the sandwiches, put the bacon strips under a hot preheated broiler or in a hot skillet and cook, turning frequently, until the bacon is crisp and golden brown. Spread the butter over the slices of bread.

5 Put two bacon strips on the bottom pieces of bread, season with pepper to taste, and spoon the tomato sauce over the bacon. Top with the other slice of bread and serve immediately.

EGG & BACON PIE

Serves: 4–6

Prep: 25–30 minutes, Cook: 50–55 minutes
plus chilling and cooling

Ingredients

Pastry dough

1 stick salted butter

1⅔ cups all-purpose flour,
plus extra for dusting

1–2 tablespoons cold water

Filling

1 stick butter

1 small onion,
finely chopped

4 lean bacon strips, diced

½ cup shredded
cheddar cheese

2 eggs, beaten

1¼ cups light cream

pepper

Method

1 For the dough, rub the butter into the flour with your fingertips until the mixture resembles fine bread crumbs. Stir in just enough water to bind the mixture to a firm dough. Roll out on a lightly floured surface and use to line a 9-inch loose-bottom round tart pan. Prick the bottom all over with a fork. Chill for at least 10 minutes.

2 Preheat the oven to 400°F. Line the pastry shell with parchment paper and pie weights or dried beans, place on a baking sheet, and bake for 10 minutes. Remove the paper and weights and bake for an additional 10 minutes.

3 For the filling, melt the butter in a skillet and sauté the onion and bacon for about 5 minutes, until the onion is softened and lightly browned. Spread the mixture in the pastry shell and sprinkle with half the cheese. Beat together the eggs and cream and season with pepper. Pour into the pastry shell and sprinkle with the remaining cheese.

4 Reduce the oven temperature to 375°F. Bake the pie for 25–30 minutes, or until golden brown and just set. Cool for 10 minutes before turning out.

HAMBURGERS

Serves: 4   **Prep: 20 minutes**   **Cook: 20 minutes**

Ingredients

1½ pounds fresh ground beef chuck

1 red bell pepper, seeded and finely chopped

1 garlic clove, finely chopped

2 small red chiles, seeded and finely chopped

1 tablespoon chopped fresh basil

½ teaspoon ground cumin

salt and pepper

fresh basil sprigs, to garnish

hamburger buns, to serve

Method

1 Preheat the broiler to medium–high. Put the beef, red bell pepper, garlic, chiles, chopped basil, and cumin into a bowl.

2 Mix until well combined and season to taste with salt and pepper.

3 Using your hands, form the mixture into four patties. Place the patties under the preheated broiler and cook for 5–8 minutes.

4 Using a spatula, turn the burgers and cook on the other side for 5–8 minutes. To make sure the burgers are cooked through, cut into the middle to check that the meat is no longer pink. Any juices that run out should be clear and piping hot with visible steam rising.

5 Garnish with basil sprigs and serve immediately in burger buns.

FRENCH TOAST

Serves: 2   **Prep: 15 minutes**   **Cook: 5 minutes**

Ingredients

1 extra-large egg

¼ cup milk or light cream

2 slices day-old
thick white bread

2 tablespoons butter

Method

1 Break the egg into a shallow bowl and whisk well. Stir in the milk.

2 Dip the bread into the egg mixture and coat both sides well.

3 Heat half of the butter in a skillet over medium heat and gently cook one piece of egg-soaked bread for about 1 minute on each side, or until golden brown and crispy. Be careful not to let it burn. Remove the French toast from the pan and keep warm. Melt the remaining butter and repeat with the other piece of bread. Serve immediately.

MEATBALLS

Serves: 4

Prep: 30 minutes, plus cooling

Cook: 35 minutes

Ingredients

1 tablespoon olive oil

1 small onion, finely chopped

2 garlic cloves, finely chopped

2 fresh thyme sprigs, finely chopped

1½ pounds fresh ground round beef

½ cup fresh bread crumbs

1 egg, lightly beaten

salt and pepper

Sauce

1 onion, cut into wedges

3 red bell peppers, halved and seeded

1 (14-ounce) can diced tomatoes

1 bay leaf

Method

1 Heat the oil in a skillet. Add the onion and garlic and cook over low heat for 5 minutes, or until soft. Put into a bowl with the thyme, ground beef, bread crumbs, and egg. Season to taste with salt and pepper, mix thoroughly, and shape into 20 golf ball-size balls.

2 Heat a large skillet over low–medium heat. Add the meatballs and cook, stirring gently for 15 minutes. To make sure the meat is cooked through, cut into the middle to check that there are no remaining traces of pink.

3 Meanwhile, for the sauce, preheat the broiler. Cook the onion wedges and bell pepper halves under the preheated broiler, turning often, for 10 minutes, until the pepper skins are blistered and charred.

4 Put the bell peppers into a plastic bag, tie the top, and let cool. Set the onion wedges aside. Peel off the pepper skins and coarsely chop the flesh. Put the pepper flesh into a food processor with the onion wedges and tomatoes. Process to a smooth puree and season to taste with salt and pepper.

5 Pour into a saucepan with the bay leaf and bring to a boil. Reduce the heat and simmer, stirring occasionally, for 10 minutes. Remove and discard the bay leaf. Serve the sauce immediately with the meatballs.

FRIED CHICKEN WINGS

Serves: 4   **Prep: 25 minutes**   **Cook: 25 minutes**

Ingredients

12 chicken wings
1 egg
¼ cup milk
½ cup all-purpose flour
1 teaspoon paprika
2 cups dried bread crumbs
4 tablespoons butter
salt and pepper

Method

1 Preheat the oven to 425°F. Separate each chicken wing into three pieces, discarding the bony tip. Beat the egg with the milk in a shallow dish.

2 Combine the flour, paprika, and salt and pepper to taste in a shallow dish. Put the bread crumbs into another dish. Dip the chicken in the egg mixture, drain, and then roll in the flour.

3 Shake off any excess, then roll the chicken wings in the bread crumbs, gently pressing them onto the surface and shaking off any excess crumbs.

4 Put the butter into a wide, shallow roasting pan and put into the preheated oven to melt.

5 Place the chicken in the pan skin side down.

6 Bake for 10 minutes on each side. To make sure the wings are cooked through, cut into the middle to check that there are no remaining traces of pink or red. Any juices that run out should be clear and piping hot with visible steam rising.

7 Transfer the chicken to a serving plate and serve.

BEEF IN STOUT WITH HERB DUMPLINGS

Serves: 6

Prep: 35 minutes

Cook: 2 hours 40 minutes

Ingredients

Stew

2 tablespoons sunflower oil

2 large onions, thinly sliced

8 carrots, sliced

¼ cup all-purpose flour

2¾ pounds boneless beef chuck, cut into cubes

2 cups stout

2 teaspoons packed light brown sugar

2 bay leaves

1 tablespoon chopped fresh thyme

salt and pepper

Herb dumplings

1 cup all-purpose flour

1 teaspoon baking powder

pinch of salt

¼ cup suet or lard

2 tablespoons chopped fresh parsley, plus extra to garnish

about ¼ cup water

Method

1 Preheat the oven to 325°F. Heat the oil in a flameproof casserole dish or Dutch oven. Add the onions and carrots and cook over low heat, stirring occasionally, for 5 minutes, or until the onions are softened. Meanwhile, put the flour into a plastic bag and season well with salt and pepper. Add the beef to the bag, tie the top, and shake well to coat. Do this in batches, if necessary. Reserve any remaining seasoned flour.

2 Remove the onions and carrots from the casserole with a slotted spoon and reserve. Add the beef to the casserole, in batches, and cook, stirring frequently, until browned all over. Return all the meat and the onions and carrots to the casserole and sprinkle in the reserved seasoned flour. Pour in the stout and add the sugar, bay leaves, and thyme. Bring to a boil, cover, and cook in the preheated oven for 1¾ hours.

3 To make the herb dumplings, sift the flour, baking powder, and salt into a bowl. Stir in the suet and parsley and add enough of the water to make a soft dough. Shape into small balls between the palms of your hands. Add to the casserole and return to the oven for 30 minutes. Remove the bay leaves and discard. Serve immediately, sprinkled with parsley.

BOILED EGGS WITH TOAST

Serves: 2   **Prep: 15 minutes**   **Cook: 10 minutes**

Ingredients

4 extra-large eggs
salt and pepper

Toast

crusty white loaf,
sliced and cut into
thick strips, buttered

Method

1 Bring a small saucepan of water to a boil; it is best to use a small saucepan to prevent the eggs from rolling around and cracking. The water should be deep enough to cover the eggs.

2 Gently lower the eggs into the water, using a long-handle spoon or ladle. Keep the water at a gentle simmer and cook for 3–4 minutes if you prefer a runny yolk and set white, or 4–5 minutes if you prefer a firmer egg.

3 Remove the eggs from the pan, using a slotted spoon, drain quickly on paper towels, and place in egg cups.

4 Season with salt and pepper to taste and serve immediately with the toast.

HOME COMFORTS

SMOKED COD CHOWDER

Serves: 4   **Prep: 20 minutes**   **Cook: 35 minutes**

Ingredients

2 tablespoons butter

1 onion, finely chopped

1 small celery stalk, finely diced

Yukon gold or red-skinned potatoes, diced

1 carrot, diced

1¼ cups boiling water

12 ounces smoked cod fillets, skinned and cut into bite-size pieces

1¼ cups milk

salt and pepper

fresh flat-leaf parsley sprigs, to garnish

Method

1 Melt the butter in a large saucepan over low heat, add the onion and celery, and cook, stirring frequently, for 5 minutes, or until soft but not brown.

2 Add the potatoes, carrot, water, and salt and pepper to taste. Bring to a boil, then reduce the heat and simmer for 10 minutes, or until the vegetables are tender. Add the fish to the chowder and cook for an additional 10 minutes.

3 Pour in the milk and heat gently. Taste and adjust the seasoning, adding salt and pepper, if necessary. Ladle into warm bowls and serve, garnished with parsley sprigs.

HOME COMFORTS

STEAK & ENGLISH MUSTARD SANDWICH

Serves: 2   **Prep: 20–25 minutes**   **Cook: 25–30 minutes, plus resting**

Ingredients

1 tablespoon butter

2 tablespoons olive oil

1 onion, halved and thinly sliced

½ teaspoon packed light brown sugar

2 (6-ounce) top sirloin steaks, about ¾ inch thick

1 teaspoon coarsely ground black pepper

¼ cup mayonnaise

2 teaspoons prepared English mustard

4 thick slices crusty white bread

1 cup arugula or other peppery greens

salt and pepper

Method

1 Heat the butter and half the oil in a skillet and sauté the sliced onion gently for 10 minutes, until softened. Season with salt and pepper and sprinkle with the sugar. Increase the heat a little and continue cooking for an additional 5 minutes, until golden and caramelized.

2 Heat a cast iron, ridged grill pan until hot. Drizzle the remaining oil over the steaks, coat with the black pepper, and season lightly with salt. Add the steaks to the pan and cook over high heat for 3–5 minutes on each side, until cooked to your preference. Remove the steaks from the pan, cover, and let rest in a warm place for 10 minutes.

3 Mix together the mayonnaise and mustard and spread thickly over two slices of the bread. Top with the arugula. Using a sharp knife, thinly slice the steaks on an angle. Pile the steak on top of the arugula and top with the caramelized onions. Sandwich with the remaining slices of bread and serve immediately.

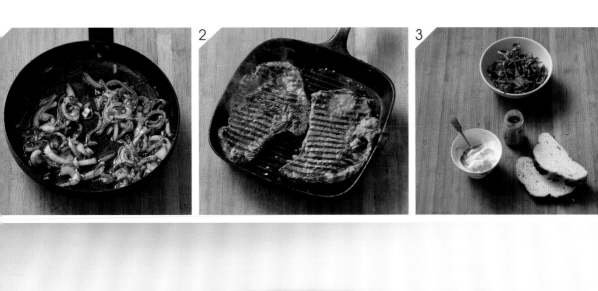

MUSHROOM & ONION QUICHE

Serves: 4

Prep: 25 minutes, plus chilling and cooling

Cook: 1 hour 20 minutes

Ingredients

butter, for greasing

1 ready-to-bake rolled dough pie crust, thawed if frozen

flour, for dusting

Filling

4 tablespoons unsalted butter

3 red onions, halved and sliced

12 ounces mixed wild mushrooms, such as porcini, chanterelles, and morels

2 teaspoons chopped fresh thyme

1 egg

2 egg yolks

½ cup heavy cream

salt and pepper

Method

1 Preheat the oven to 375°F. Lightly grease a 9-inch loose-bottom tart pan. Roll out the dough on a lightly floured work surface and use to line the pan. Line the pastry shell with parchment paper and fill with pie weights or dried beans. Chill in the refrigerator for 30 minutes. Bake in the preheated oven for 25 minutes. Remove the paper and weights and cool on a wire rack. Reduce the oven temperature to 350°F.

2 To make the filling, melt the butter in a large, heavy skillet over low heat. Add the onions, cover, and cook, stirring occasionally, for 20 minutes. Add the mushrooms and thyme and cook, stirring occasionally, for an additional 10 minutes. Spoon into the pastry shell and place the pan on a baking sheet.

3 Lightly beat the egg, egg yolks, cream, and salt and pepper to taste in a bowl. Pour the egg mixture over the mushroom mixture. Bake in the oven for 20 minutes, or until the filling is set and golden. Serve hot or at room temperature.

POTATO & CABBAGE CAKES

Serves: 4   **Prep: 30 minutes**   **Cook: 40–45 minutes**

Ingredients

4 russet potatoes
(about 1 pound),
cut into chunks

4 tablespoons butter

3 tablespoons hot milk

1 small head of
green cabbage

¼ cup olive oil

1 onion, thinly sliced

salt and pepper

Method

1 Bring a large saucepan of lightly salted water to a boil, add the potatoes, and cook for 15–20 minutes. Drain well and mash with a potato masher until smooth. Season with salt and pepper, add the butter and milk, and stir well.

2 Cut the cabbage into quarters, remove the core, and finely shred the leaves.

3 Heat half of the oil in a large skillet, add the onion, and sauté until soft. Add the cabbage to the pan and stir-fry for 2–3 minutes, until soft. Season with salt and pepper, add the mashed potatoes, and mix together well.

4 Press the mixture firmly into the skillet and let cook over high heat for 4–5 minutes, until the bottom is crispy. Place a plate over the pan and invert the pan so that the potato cake falls onto the plate. Add the remaining oil to the pan, reheat, and slip the cake back into the pan with the uncooked side down.

5 Continue to cook for an additional 5 minutes, until the bottom is crispy. Turn out onto a warm plate, cut into wedges, and serve immediately.

HOME COMFORTS

POT ROAST

Serves: 6　　**Prep: 30–35 minutes**　　**Cook: 3 hours 40 minutes**

Ingredients

4–5 potatoes, cut into large chunks

2½ tablespoons all-purpose flour

1 (3½-pound) rolled beef brisket

2 tablespoons vegetable oil

2 tablespoons butter

1 onion, finely chopped

2 celery stalks, diced

2 carrots, peeled and diced

1 teaspoon dill seed

1 teaspoon dried thyme

1½ cups red wine

⅔–1 cup beef broth

salt and pepper

2 tablespoons chopped fresh dill, to serve

Method

1　Bring a large saucepan of lightly salted water to a boil. Add the potatoes, bring back to a boil, and cook for 10 minutes. Drain and set aside. Preheat the oven to 275°F. Mix 2 tablespoons of the flour with 1 teaspoon salt and ¼ teaspoon pepper in a large shallow dish. Dip the meat in the flour to coat.

2　Heat the oil in a flameproof casserole dish or Dutch oven, add the meat, and brown. Transfer to a plate. Add half the butter to the casserole, then add the onion, celery, carrots, dill seed, and thyme and cook for 5 minutes. Return the meat and juices to the dish. Pour in the wine and enough broth to reach one-third of the way up the meat, and bring to a boil. Cover and cook in the oven for 3 hours, turning the meat every 30 minutes. Add the potatoes and more broth, if necessary, after 2 hours.

3　When ready, put the meat and vegetables onto a warm serving dish. Strain the cooking liquid to remove any solids and return to the casserole. Mix the rest of the butter and flour to a paste. Bring the cooking liquid to a boil. Whisk in the flour paste, a little at a time, whisking constantly until the sauce is smooth. Pour the sauce over the meat, sprinkle with fresh dill, and serve.

★ Variation

For a spicer dish, add ¼ teaspoon of ground allspice for a heartier pot roast.

FAMILY CELEBRATION DINNERS

ROASTED TURKEY

Serves: 8

Prep: 25–30 minutes

Cook: 3 hours 40 minutes
plus resting

Ingredients

1 pound sweet Italian sausages (casings removed)

1 (6-ounce) package turkey stuffing

1 (11-pound) turkey

3 tablespoons butter

bay leaves, sage leaves, and chives, to garnish (optional)

To serve

bread sauce or gravy

roasted potatoes

roasted vegetables

Method

1 Preheat the oven to 425°F. Cook the sausages in a skillet over medium heat, breaking them up into crumbly pieces, for about 10 minutes, until browned. Drain on paper towels and set aside.

2 Prepare the stuffing according to the package directions, then mix it with the cooked sausage. Spoon the stuffing into the neck cavity of the turkey and close the flap of skin with a toothpick. Place the bird in a large roasting pan and rub it all over with the butter. Roast in the preheated oven for 1 hour, then lower the temperature to 350°F and roast for another 2½ hours. You may need to pour off fat from the pan occasionally.

3 To check if the turkey is cooked, insert the point of a sharp knife into the thickest part of the thigh; if the juices run clear, it is ready. Transfer to a carving board, cover with aluminum foil, and let rest.

4 Garnish the turkey with bay, sage, and chives, if using. Carve and serve with warm bread sauce or gravy and roasted potatoes and vegetables.

★ Variation

Bake any extra stuffing in a separate baking dish; unlike the stuffing in the bird, it will be safe to reheat for leftovers.

FAMILY CELEBRATION DINNERS

GLAZED HAM IN CIDER

Serves: 6–8

Prep: 30 minutes, plus cooling

Cook: 4½ hours

Ingredients

1 (9-pound) country ham

1 apple, cored and chopped

1 onion, chopped

1¼ cups hard apple cider or apple juice

6 black peppercorns

1 bouquet garni (sprigs of parsley, bay leaf, and thyme tied together)

1 bay leaf

about 50 cloves

¼ cup raw brown sugar

Method

1 Put the ham into a large saucepan and add enough cold water to cover. Bring to a boil and skim off any foam that rises to the surface. Reduce the heat and simmer for 30 minutes.

2 Drain the ham and return to the saucepan. Add the apple, onion, cider, peppercorns, bouquet garni, bay leaf, and a few of the cloves. Pour in enough fresh water to cover and bring back to a boil. Cover and simmer for 3 hours 20 minutes.

3 Preheat the oven to 400°F. Take the saucepan off the heat and set aside to cool slightly. Remove the ham from the cooking liquid and while it is still warm, loosen the rind with a sharp knife, then peel it off and discard.

4 Score the fat into diamond shapes and stud with the remaining cloves. Place the ham on a rack in a roasting pan and sprinkle with the sugar. Roast in the preheated oven, basting occasionally with the cooking liquid, for 20 minutes. To check it is cooked, insert the tip of a sharp knife into the center of the meat; the juices should run clear. Serve hot or cold.

POACHED SALMON

Serves: 6

Prep: 25–30 minutes,   Cook: 12–18 minutes
plus cooling and standing

Ingredients

1 (8-pound) whole salmon
3 tablespoons salt
3 bay leaves
10 black peppercorns
1 onion, sliced
1 lemon, sliced
lemon wedges, to serve

Method

1 Wipe the salmon thoroughly inside and out with paper towels, then use the back of a chef's knife to remove any scales that might still be on the skin. Remove the fins with scissors and trim the tail. Some prefer to cut off the head, but it is traditionally prepared with it on.

2 Place the salmon on the two-handled rack that comes with a fish poacher, then place it in the poacher. Fill the poacher with enough cold water to cover the salmon adequately. Sprinkle with the salt, bay leaves, and peppercorns and sprinkle in the onion and lemon slices.

3 Place the poacher over low heat, over two burners, and slowly bring just to a boil. Cover and simmer gently. To serve cold, simmer for only 2 minutes, remove from the heat, and let cool in the liquid for about 2 hours with the lid on. To serve hot, simmer for 6–8 minutes and let stand in the hot water for 15 minutes before removing. Remove the fish from the poacher, skin, and serve with lemon wedges for squeezing over the fish.

MUSHROOM STROGANOFF

Serves: 4   **Prep: 15–20 minutes**   **Cook: 15–20 minutes**

Ingredients

2 tablespoons butter

1 onion, finely chopped

1 pound closed-cup mushrooms, quartered

1 teaspoon tomato paste

1 teaspoon whole-grain mustard

⅔ cup crème fraîche

1 teaspoon paprika, plus extra to garnish

salt and pepper

fresh flat-leaf parsley sprigs, to garnish

Method

1 Heat the butter in a large, heavy skillet. Add the onion and sauté gently for 5–10 minutes, until soft.

2 Add the mushrooms to the skillet and stir-fry for a few minutes, until they begin to soften.

3 Stir in the tomato paste and mustard, then add the crème fraîche. Cook gently, stirring constantly for 5 minutes.

4 Stir in the paprika and season to taste with salt and pepper.

5 Garnish with extra paprika and parsley sprigs and serve immediately.

BEEF WELLINGTON

Serves: 6

Prep: 35 minutes, plus cooling and chilling

Cook: 1 hour–1 hour 20 minutes

Ingredients

2 tablespoons olive or vegetable oil

3¼ pounds beef tenderloin, trimmed of fat and sinew

4 tablespoons butter

2 cups chopped mushrooms

2 garlic cloves, crushed

5½ ounces smooth liver pâté

few drops of truffle oil (optional)

1 tablespoon finely chopped fresh parsley

2 teaspoon English mustard

1 (1-pound) package ready-to-bake puff pastry

1 egg, lightly beaten

salt and pepper

roasted root vegetables, to serve

Method

1 Put a large skillet over high heat and add the olive oil. Rub salt and pepper to taste into the beef and sear quickly all over in the pan. (This method produces a rare version. If you want it less rare, roast it at 425°F for 20 minutes at this stage.) Set aside to cool.

2 Heat the butter in a skillet over medium heat, add the mushrooms, and sauté for 5 minutes. Reduce the heat, add the garlic, and sauté for another 5 minutes. Put the mushrooms and garlic into a bowl, add the pâté, truffle oil, if using, and parsley, and beat with a fork. Let cool.

3 Rub the mustard into the seared beef. Roll out the pastry into a rectangle large enough to wrap the whole beef with some to spare. Spread the mushroom paste in the middle of the pastry, leaving a 2-inch gap between the paste and the edge of the pastry, and lay the beef on top. Brush the edges of the pastry with beaten egg and fold it over, edges overlapping, and across the meat to completely enclose it.

4 Preheat the oven to 425°F. Place the wrapped beef in a roasting pan with the seam underneath and brush with beaten egg. Let chill in the refrigerator for 15 minutes, then transfer to the preheated oven and bake for 50 minutes. Check after 30 minutes; if the pastry looks golden brown, cover with aluminum foil to prevent it from burning. Serve immediately with roasted root vegetables.

SHRIMP COCKTAIL WITH QUAIL EGGS

Serves: 4   **Prep: 25 minutes, plus cooling**   **Cook: 10 minutes**

Ingredients

8 quail eggs

⅓ cup mayonnaise

3 tablespoons Greek-style yogurt

2 tablespoons ketchup

dash of Tabasco sauce

2 teaspoon lime juice

1½ cups peppery greens

2-inch piece of cucumber, finely diced

1 small ripe avocado, peeled and thinly sliced

8 ounces cooked jumbo shrimp, peeled and tails left intact

salt and pepper

lime wedges and fresh dill sprigs, to garnish

Method

1 Bring a small saucepan of water to a boil, then reduce to a simmer. Gently lower the quail eggs into the water and simmer for 5 minutes. Drain and cool under running cold water. Once cold, shell and set aside.

2 Put the mayonnaise, yogurt, ketchup, Tabasco sauce, and lime juice into a bowl and mix together thoroughly. Season to taste with salt and pepper.

3 Divide the greens among four large wine or cocktail glasses. Sprinkle with the diced cucumber. Halve the eggs and arrange on top of the salad with the avocado slices and shrimp (reserving eight shrimp to garnish).

4 Spoon the mayonnaise dressing over the top. Serve garnished with the reserved shrimp, lime wedges, and sprigs of dill.

FAMILY CELEBRATION DINNERS

POTTED CRAB

Serves: 4

Prep: 25 minutes, plus cooling and chilling

Cook: 2-3 minutes

Ingredients

(6-ounce) cans crabmeat or 1⅓ cups cooked crabmeat

¼ teaspoon cayenne pepper

2 tablespoons lemon juice

1¼ sticks butter, softened

salt and pepper

fresh parsley sprigs, to garnish

lemon wedges and Melba toast or crusty bread, to serve

Method

1 Put the crabmeat into a bowl and break up with a fork. Stir in the cayenne pepper and lemon juice and season with salt and pepper.

2 Add 6 tablespoons of the butter and beat until thoroughly combined. Divide the mixture among four ½-cup ramekins (individual ceramic dishes) and level the surface.

3 Put the remaining butter into a small saucepan and heat gently until melted. Cool for 5 minutes, then skim off any white froth with a spoon. Pour the melted butter in a thin stream over the top of each dish of crab mixture to cover evenly, leaving any sediment in the bottom of the pan. Let stand until cold, then place the ramekins in the refrigerator for about 2 hours until the butter is firm.

4 Remove the ramekins from the refrigerator about 30 minutes before serving. Garnish with parsley sprigs and serve with lemon wedges and Melba toast or crusty bread.

SEA TROUT WITH CIDER & CREAM SAUCE

Serves: 8–10　　　**Prep: 35 minutes**　　　**Cook: 1½ hours**

Ingredients

oil, for brushing

1 (7½–7¾-pound) whole sea trout or salmon, gutted

small bunch parsley, plus a few extra sprigs to garnish

2 fresh bay leaves

sea salt flakes

pepper

1 leek, halved lengthwise and sliced

2 lemons, thinly sliced

4 tablespoons salted butter

1 cup dry hard cider or apple juice

1 cup light cream

3 tablespoons chopped fresh tarragon or dill

boiled new potatoes and peas, to serve

Method

1　Preheat the oven to 350°F. Line a roasting pan with aluminum foil large enough to loosely enclose the fish in a sealed package. Brush the inside of the foil with oil. Remove the head, tail, and fins from the fish. Place the fish on the foil and stuff the cavity with the parsley and bay leaves. Rub all over with sea salt flakes and black pepper. Arrange the leek slices and half the lemon slices over the fish, and dot with the butter. Gather up the foil and pour the cider around the fish. Seal the foil well, leaving a small vent at the top.

2　Place the fish package in its roasting pan in the preheated oven and bake for 1¼ hours, or until the thickest part of the flesh looks opaque when pierced with the tip of a knife. Open the foil and carefully slide the fish onto a warm serving plate, discarding the parsley, bay leaves, lemon, and leek. Keep warm.

3　Transfer the juices from the foil into the pan, along with any that flow from the fish, and place on the stove over medium–high heat. Stir in the cream and tarragon, then simmer briskly for 10–15 minutes, until slightly thickened. Check the seasoning and pour into a small bowl.

4　Remove the skin from the top of the fish. Garnish with the remaining lemon slices and parsley sprigs. Serve with the sauce, new potatoes, and peas.

PORK TENDERLOIN WITH ROASTED RHUBARB

Serves: 4 **Prep: 30 minutes** **Cook: 55–60 minutes,**
plus resting

Ingredients

1¾ pounds boneless pork loin

olive oil

1 teaspoon sea salt flakes

½ teaspoon black pepper

10 small sprigs of rosemary

½ cup chicken broth

3–4 pink rhubarb stalks, trimmed and sliced diagonally into 1½-inch lengths

1 tablespoon honey

Method

1 Preheat the oven to 375°F. Using the tip of a sharp knife, score the fat, but not the flesh, of the pork at ½-inch intervals. Tie the meat with kitchen string to form a neat roll. You can ask your butcher to do both of these.

2 Put the meat into a small roasting pan. Rub with oil and then with the sea salt and black pepper, rubbing them in well. Insert the rosemary sprigs into the slits in the fat. Roast in the preheated oven for 40 minutes.

3 Pour in the broth. Arrange the rhubarb around the meat and drizzle with the honey. Roast for an additional 10–15 minutes, until the rhubarb is tender and starting to brown at the edges.

4 Transfer the pork and rhubarb to a warm serving plate, reserving the pan juices. Make a tent over the meat with aluminum foil and let rest for 10 minutes in a warm place.

5 Place the roasting pan on the stove over medium-high heat. Let simmer rapidly to reduce the pan juices, including any that have flowed from the meat, for 3–4 minutes, until slightly thickened. Check the seasoning, strain into a small bowl, and serve with the meat.

ROASTED GOOSE WITH APPLE STUFFING & CIDER GRAVY

Serves: 4–5

Prep: 45–55 minutes, plus drying and cooling

Cook: 5¼ hours, plus resting

Ingredients

1 (9-pound) goose, with the giblets (the neck, heart, and gizzard) and lumps of fat in the cavity reserved, and wing tips and leg tips cut off and reserved

1 onion, coarsely chopped

1 celery stalk, coarsely chopped

1 large carrot, coarsely chopped

handful of parsley

2–3 thyme sprigs

2 fresh bay leaves

½ teaspoon black peppercorns

2 small firm apples

1 cup dry hard cider or apple juice

2 tablespoons apple cider vinegar

2 tablespoons all-purpose flour

salt and pepper

Method

1 Prick the goose all over with a fork and put into a colander. Douse with plenty of boiling water, then pat dry with paper towels. Season inside the cavity with salt and pepper, and rub salt all over the skin. Let dry.

2 To make the stuffing, heat a pat of the goose fat in a skillet over medium heat, add the onion, and sauté until soft. Add the bacon, potatoes, apples, sage, thyme, salt, and pepper. Gently cook, covered, for 20 minutes, until the apples are soft. Add the liver, parsley, and lemon zest, and cook for 5 minutes. Spread out the stuffing in a wide bowl and let cool.

3 Meanwhile, make a broth. Put the reserved wing and leg tips and giblets into a saucepan. Add the vegetables, herbs and peppercorns. Pour in enough cold water to just cover. Slowly bring to a boil, covered, reduce the heat, and simmer with the lid askew for 2 hours.

4 Preheat the oven to 400°F. Spoon the stuffing into the goose cavity. Insert an apple at each end to hold the stuffing in place and seal the flaps with toothpicks. Truss the wings and legs with string. Put the goose into a roasting pan and cook for 30 minutes, then pour off the fat. Reduce the

Apple stuffing

3 onions, chopped

4 unsmoked bacon strips, chopped

4 russet potatoes (about 1 pound), cut into ½-inch dice

3 Granny Smith or other cooking apples, quartered, cored, peeled, and coarsely chopped

1½ tablespoons chopped fresh sage

1 tablespoon chopped fresh thyme

½ teaspoon sea salt

¼ teaspoon black pepper

4 ounces goose liver, chopped

2 tablespoons chopped fresh parsley

finely grated zest of 1 lemon

temperature to 350°F. Cover the goose loosely with aluminum foil and cook for 1½ hours, pouring off the fat two more times at 30-minute intervals. Add some water if the pan looks dry. Remove the foil and roast for 30 minutes, until the juices run clear when the thickest part of the thigh is pierced with the tip of a sharp knife. Lift the goose onto a warm plate, cover with foil, and let rest for 20 minutes.

5 To make the gravy, strain 2 cups of the pan juices and blot up any fat that rises. Pour off the liquid and fat in the pan. Stir in the cider and vinegar, heat over medium heat, scraping up any sediment in the pan. Add the flour and stir for a minute, until blended. Pour in the strained juices. Bring to a boil, simmer for 5 minutes, and strain.

6 Slice the apples and arrange around the goose. Carve the goose and serve with the sliced apples, stuffing, and cider gravy.

PRIME RIB OF BEEF AU JUS

Serves: 8

Prep: 20-25 minutes, plus standing

Cook: 2 -2½ hours, plus resting

Ingredients

6 pound rib of beef

4 tablespoons butter, softened

1½ teaspoons sea salt flakes

1 tablespoon ground black pepper

2 tablespoons flour

4 cups beef broth

thyme sprigs, to garnish

roasted potatoes and vegetables, to serve

Method

1 Put the beef, bone side down, in a deep flameproof roasting pan or Dutch oven. Rub the entire surface of the meat with butter, and coat evenly with the salt and black pepper.

2 Let the beef stand to reach room temperature for 1 hour. Preheat the oven to 450°F. Put the meat into the preheated oven and roast, uncovered, for 20 minutes to sear the outside of the roast.

3 Reduce the heat to 325°F and roast for 15 minutes per 1 pound of meat for medium-rare (plus or minus 15 minutes for well done and rare respectively). Transfer the meat to a large plate and cover with aluminum foil. Let rest for 30 minutes before serving.

4 Pour off all but 2 tablespoons of the fat from the pan and place the roasting pan over medium heat. Add the flour to the roasting pan and simmer, stirring with a wooden spoon for 1 minute to form a thick paste. Pour in a ladleful of beef broth, bring to a boil, stirring and scraping all the caramelized beef sediment from the bottom of the pan. Repeat with the remaining broth, a ladleful at a time. Simmer for 10 minutes.

5 Serve the beef with the "jus" accompanied by roasted potatoes and vegetables and garnished with thyme.

CHICKEN LIVER PÂTÉ

Serves: 6

Prep: 25 minutes, plus cooling and chilling

Cook: 15 minutes

Ingredients

1¾ sticks butter

8 ounces trimmed chicken livers, thawed if frozen

2 tablespoons medium red wine or brandy

1½ teaspoons chopped fresh sage

1 garlic clove, coarsely chopped

⅔ cup heavy cream

salt and pepper

fresh bay leaves or sage leaves, to garnish

Melba toast, to serve

Method

1 Melt 3 tablespoons of the butter in a large, heavy skillet. Add the chicken livers and cook over medium heat for 4 minutes on each side. They should be brown on the outside but still pink in the center. Transfer to a food processor and process until finely chopped.

2 Stir the red wine into the skillet, scraping up any sediment with a wooden spoon, then add to the food processor with the chopped sage, garlic, and 1 stick of the remaining butter. Process until smooth. Add the cream, season to taste, and process until thoroughly combined and smooth. Spoon the pâté into a dish or ramekins (individual ceramic dishes), smooth the surface, and let cool completely.

3 Melt the remaining butter in a small saucepan, let cool for 5 minutes, skim off any white froth, then spoon over the surface of the pâté, leaving any sediment in the saucepan. Garnish with herb leaves, let cool, then cover and chill in the refrigerator. Serve with Melba toast.

FAMILY CELEBRATION DINNERS

GLAZED BEET & EGG SOURDOUGH TOASTS

Serves: 2–4   **Prep: 25 minutes**   **Cook: 12–15 minutes**

Ingredients

4 eggs

10 cooked beets

2 teaspoons sugar, or to taste

2 tablespoons apple cider vinegar, or to taste

4 slices sourdough bread

⅓ cup olive oil

tablespoon Dijon mustard

3 tablespoons chopped fresh dill

salt and pepper

Method

1. Cook the eggs in a saucepan of boiling water for 8 minutes, then drain, shell, and chop them. Set aside. Cut the beets into small dice and put into a small bowl. Mix in half the sugar and 1 teaspoon of the vinegar and season to taste with salt and pepper.

2. Preheat the broiler to medium–high. Brush the bread with a little of the oil and toast under the preheated broiler for 2–3 minutes, until crisp and golden.

3. Meanwhile, drizzle 1 teaspoon of the remaining oil over the beets. Whisk together the remaining vinegar and sugar with the mustard and salt and pepper to taste. Gradually whisk in the remaining oil to make a thick dressing. Stir in the dill and taste for seasoning—it should be sweet and mustardy, with a sharpness—add more sugar or vinegar, if desired.

4. Turn the bread over, stir the beets, and spread over the slices right up to the crusts. Glaze the beets under the broiler for 2–3 minutes, until browned in places.

5. Cut the slices in half or quarters and top with the reserved chopped egg. Drizzle with a little dressing and serve immediately.

FAMILY CELEBRATION DINNERS

GARLIC & HERB LANGOUSTINES

Serves: 2

Prep: 25 minutes,
plus marinating

Cook: 5–6 minutes

Ingredients

12 raw langoustines
crayfish, or large shrimp in
their shells

juice of ½ lemon

2 garlic cloves, crushed

3 tablespoons chopped
fresh parsley

1 tablespoon chopped
fresh dill

3 tablespoons butter,
softened

salt and pepper

lemon wedges
and crusty bread,
to serve

Method

1 Rinse the langoustines and set aside.

2 Mix the lemon juice with the garlic, herbs, and butter to form a paste. Season well with salt and pepper. Spread the paste over the langoustines and let marinate for 30 minutes. Meanwhile, preheat the broiler to medium.

3 Cook the langoustines under the preheated broiler for 5–6 minutes. Alternatively, cook the langoustines in a skillet until they turn pink and are cooked through. Turn out onto warm plates and pour the pan juices over them. Serve immediately with lemon wedges and crusty bread.

FAMILY CELEBRATION DINNERS

DEVILS & ANGELS ON HORSEBACK

Makes: 32   **Prep: 25–30 minutes**   **Cook: 10–15 minutes**

Ingredients

Devils

rindless lean bacon strips

8 canned anchovy fillets in oil, drained

16 whole blanched almonds

16 pitted prunes

Angels

rindless lean bacon strips

16 smoked oysters, drained if canned

sprigs of fresh thyme, to garnish

Method

1 Preheat the oven to 400°F.

2 For the devils, cut each bacon strip lengthwise in half and gently stretch with the back of a knife. Cut each anchovy fillet lengthwise in half. Wrap half an anchovy around each almond and press them into the cavity in the prunes, where the pits have been removed. Wrap a strip of bacon around each prune and secure with a toothpick.

3 For the angels, cut each bacon strip lengthwise in half and gently stretch with the back of a knife. Wrap a bacon strip around each oyster and secure with a toothpick.

4 Put the devils and angels onto a baking sheet and cook in the preheated oven for 10–15 minutes, until sizzling hot and the bacon is cooked. Garnish with sprigs of fresh thyme and serve hot.

FAMILY CELEBRATION DINNERS

LASAGNE

Serves: 4   **Prep: 25–30 minutes   Cook: 1 hour 25 minutes**

Ingredients

2 tablespoons olive oil

2 ounces pancetta, chopped

1 onion, chopped

1 garlic clove, finely chopped

8 ounces ground round beef

2 celery stalks, chopped

2 carrots, chopped

pinch of sugar

½ teaspoon dried oregano

1 (14-ounce) can diced tomatoes

2 teaspoon Dijon mustard

2 cups prepared cheese sauce

8 ounces oven-ready lasagna noodles

1⅓ cups freshly grated Parmesan cheese, plus extra for sprinkling

salt and pepper

Method

1 Preheat the oven to 375°F. Heat the oil in a large, heavy saucepan. Add the pancetta and cook over medium heat, stirring occasionally, for 3 minutes.

2 Add the onion and garlic and sauté, stirring occasionally, for 5 minutes, or until soft.

3 Add the ground beef and cook, breaking it up with a wooden spoon, until brown all over with no remaining traces of pink. Stir in the celery and carrots and cook for 5 minutes

4 Season to taste with salt and pepper. Add the sugar, oregano, and tomatoes and their can juices. Bring to a boil, reduce the heat, and simmer for 30 minutes.

5 Meanwhile, stir the mustard into the cheese sauce. In a large, rectangular ovenproof dish, make alternate layers of meat sauce, lasagna noodles, and Parmesan cheese.

6 Pour the cheese sauce over the layers, covering them completely, and sprinkle with Parmesan cheese. Bake in the preheated oven for 30 minutes, or until golden brown and bubbling. Serve immediately.

CROWN OF ROASTED LAMB

Serves: 6

Prep: 30 minutes, plus cooling

Cook: 2¼–2½ hours, plus resting

Ingredients

3½–pound crown of lamb

2 tablespoons olive oil

salt and pepper

Stuffing

½ cup long-grain rice

2 tablespoons vegetable oil

1 onion, finely chopped

2 celery stalks, finely chopped

2 garlic cloves, crushed

3 tablespoons shelled pistachios

zest of 1 lemon, plus juice of ½ lemon

2 tablespoons finely chopped mint

2 tablespoons finely chopped parsley

⅔ cup raisins

Method

1 Calculate the cooking time of the lamb by allowing 25 minutes per 1 pound plus 25 minutes for medium, or 30 minutes per 1 pound plus 30 minutes for well done. Put the crown into a deep roasting pan, brush the outside with the oil, and season with salt and pepper. Preheat the oven to 350°F.

2 To make the stuffing, cook the rice according to the package directions until tender but still firm to the bite. Drain and cool. Heat the oil in a skillet and sauté the onion and celery for 4–5 minutes. Add the garlic and cook for another 1 minute, until softened but not browned. Stir into the cooled rice, together with the pistachios, lemon zest and juice, herbs, and raisins.

3 Fill the center of the crown with the stuffing, cover the ends of the bones with aluminum foil to prevent them from burning, then cover the whole crown with foil. Roast for the calculated time, removing the foil for the last 10–15 minutes. At the end of the cooking time, remove from the oven, lift out of the pan, cover completely with foil, and let rest for 20 minutes. Serve with the stuffing.

GAME PIE

Serves: 6

Prep: 35 minutes, plus cooling

Cook: 2–2½ hours

Ingredients

2 tablespoons sunflower oil

1¾ pounds boneless mixed game (such as venison, rabbit, and pheasant), cut into 1-inch cubes

8 ounces shallots, halved

1 garlic clove, chopped

4 ounces smoked bacon, diced

8 carrots, chopped

2 tablespoons flour, plus extra for dusting

1¼ cups chicken broth

1 cup red wine

2 tablespoons red currant or grape jelly

few sprigs of fresh thyme

1 (1-pound) package ready-to-bake puff pastry, thawed if frozen

salt and pepper

beaten egg, to glaze

Method

1 Heat half of the oil in a large flameproof casserole dish or Dutch oven. Cook the game meat, in batches, until browned, then remove with a slotted spoon and set aside. Add the rest of the oil to the dish and sauté the shallots, garlic, bacon, and carrots for 10 minutes, stirring, until browned.

2 Add the flour to the dish and cook for 1 minute, then stir in the broth, red wine, and jelly and bring to a boil. Return the meat to the dish with the thyme. Season with salt and pepper, cover, and simmer gently for 1–1¼ hours, until the meat is tender. Let cool for 1 hour.

3 Preheat the oven to 425°F. Transfer the game casserole to a large oval pie plate and put a pie funnel into the center of the dish. Dampen the rim of the plate with cold water.

4 Roll out the pastry on a lightly floured surface to an oval 2 inches wider all around than the pie plate. Cut a 1-inch strip of pastry from the outer edge, brush with water, and use to line the rim of the dish. Brush the pastry rim with water and top with the oval pastry lid. Seal, trim, and crimp the edges and decorate the top of the pie with pastry scraps.

5 Glaze the pie with the beaten egg. Bake in the preheated oven for 30–35 minutes, until the pastry is risen and golden. Serve immediately.

1

2

BUTTERNUT SQUASH & CHESTNUT RISOTTO

Serves: 4   **Prep: 25–30 minutes   Cook: 40–45 minutes**

Ingredients

1 tablespoon olive oil

3 tablespoons butter

1 small onion, finely chopped

2 cups diced butternut squash, pumpkin, or other winter squash

2 cups cooked and shelled chestnuts

1½ cups risotto rice

⅔ cup dry white wine

1 teaspoon crumbled saffron threads (optional), dissolved in ¼ cup of the broth

4 cups simmering vegetable broth

1 cup vegetarian Parmesan-style cheese, freshly grated, plus extra for serving

salt and pepper

Method

1 Heat the oil with 2 tablespoons of the butter in a deep saucepan over medium heat until the butter has melted. Stir in the onion and butternut squash and cook, stirring occasionally, for 5 minutes, or until the onion is soft and starting to turn golden and the squash begins to brown.

2 Coarsely chop the chestnuts and add to the mixture. Stir thoroughly to coat. Reduce the heat, add the rice, and mix to coat in oil and butter. Cook, stirring constantly, for 2–3 minutes, or until the grains are translucent. Add the wine and cook, stirring constantly, for 1 minute, until it has reduced.

3 Add the saffron liquid to the rice, if using, and cook, stirring constantly, until the liquid has been absorbed. Gradually add the simmering broth, a ladleful at a time, stirring constantly. Add more liquid as the rice absorbs each addition. Increase the heat to medium so that the liquid simmers.

4 Cook for 20 minutes, or until all the liquid has been absorbed and the rice is creamy. Season to taste with salt and pepper. Remove the risotto from the heat and add the remaining butter. Mix well, then stir in the cheese until it melts. Adjust the seasoning, if necessary. Spoon the risotto onto four warm plates and serve immediately, sprinkled with grated cheese.

DUCK WITH RED WINE & BLUEBERRY SAUCE

Serves: 4

Prep: 25 minutes,
plus marinating

Cook: 15 minutes,
plus standing

Ingredients

4 duck breasts (skin left on)

4 garlic cloves, chopped

grated zest and juice of
1 orange

1 tablespoon chopped
fresh parsley

salt and pepper

selection of green
vegetables, to serve

**Red wine and
blueberry sauce**

1 cup blueberries

1 cup medium red wine

1 tablespoon red currant
or grape jelly

Method

1 Use a sharp knife to make several shallow diagonal cuts in each duck breast. Put the duck into a nonmetallic bowl with the garlic, orange zest and juice, and the parsley. Season to taste with salt and pepper and stir well. Turn the duck in the mixture until thoroughly coated. Cover the bowl with plastic wrap and let rest in the refrigerator to marinate for at least 1 hour.

2 Heat a dry, nonstick skillet over medium heat. Add the duck breasts and cook for 4 minutes, then turn them over and cook for an additional 4 minutes, or according to taste. Remove from the heat, cover the skillet, and let stand for 5 minutes.

3 To make the sauce, halfway through the cooking time, put the blueberries, red wine, and jelly into a separate saucepan. Bring to a boil. Reduce the heat and simmer for 10 minutes, then remove from the heat.

4 Slice the duck breasts and transfer to warm serving plates. Serve with the sauce poured over and accompanied by a selection of green vegetables.

BLOOD SAUSAGE WITH CARAMELIZED PEAR AND CIDER

Serves: 4   **Prep: 25 minutes**   **Cook: 35–40 minutes**

Ingredients

3 tablespoons salted butter

3 firm pears, such as Bosc, peeled, cored, and quartered lengthwise

12 ounces blood sausage (the black pudding), thickly sliced

2 shallots, chopped

½ cup chicken broth

½ cup hard dry cider or apple juice

sea salt flakes

black pepper

½ cup light cream

squeeze of lemon juice

3 tablespoons chopped fresh parsley

Method

1 Heat half of the butter in a heavy skillet. When it sizzles, sauté the pears over medium–low heat for 10 minutes, turning, until caramelized at the edges. Remove from the skillet and keep warm.

2 Add the blood sausage slices to the skillet and cook for 3 minutes on each side side, turning them carefully so that they don't disintegrate. Set aside and keep warm.

3 Pour off the fat and wipe the skillet clean with paper towels. Heat the remaining butter in the skillet, add the shallots, and cook for 3–4 minutes, until softened.

4 Pour in the broth and cider, raise the heat, and bring to a boil. Reduce the heat a little, then simmer briskly for 5–7 minutes, until reduced by half. Season with sea salt and plenty of pepper.

5 Add the cream to the skillet and simmer for about a minute, until slightly thickened.

6 Return the pear slices to the skillet, add a squeeze of lemon, and cook for an additional minute, or until heated through. Sprinkle with the parsley and serve with the blood sausage slices.

RED CABBAGE STUFFED WITH MUSHROOMS, NUTS & RICE

Serves: 4-6 **Prep: 35-40 minutes** **Cook: 1¼ hours**

Ingredients

4 tablespoons butter, plus extra for greasing

1 large head of red cabbage

juice of 2 lemons

3 tablespoons olive oil

1 onion, chopped

2 cups chopped white mushrooms

1½ cups chopped mixed nuts

3 garlic cloves, chopped

2 tablespoons chopped fresh oregano

1 cup cooked Camargue red rice or long-grain brown rice

1¼ cups vegetable broth

sea salt and pepper

Tomato sauce

(see page 82)

Method

1 Preheat the oven to 350°F. Grease a 1-quart round ovenproof dish with butter. Bring a saucepan of lightly salted water to a boil. Remove 8–10 cabbage leaves and plunge into a boiling water. Add half the lemon juice and boil for 4 minutes. Drain and pat dry. Shave off the thickest part of the stem.

2 Cut the remaining cabbage in half lengthwise, reserving half for another recipe. Cut into quarters and discard the core. Shred the leaves. Heat the oil and half the butter in a large skillet over medium heat. Add the onion and sauté for 5 minutes, until translucent.

3 Add the mushrooms, nuts, chopped cabbage, garlic, oregano, and salt and pepper to taste and cook for 5 minutes. Stir in the rice, remaining lemon juice, and half the broth and cook for an additional 2 minutes.

4 Arrange the cabbage leaves around the edge and bottom of the prepared dish, leaving no gaps. Fill with the stuffing, pressing it in well. Dot with the remaining butter. Fold over the tops of the leaves. Pour the remaining broth around the edge. Tightly cover with thick aluminum foil and bake in the preheated oven for 45–50 minutes. Meanwhile, make the tomato sauce (see steps 1–3 on page 82). Serve the cabbage in wedges, accompanied by the tomato sauce.

PERFECT ROASTED POTATOES

Serves: 8   **Prep: 20 minutes**   **Cook: 1 hour 25 minutes**

Ingredients

⅓ cup goose fat, duck fat, or olive oil

9 russet potatoes (about 2¼ pounds)

coarse sea salt

8 fresh rosemary sprigs, to garnish

Method

1 Preheat the oven to 450°F. Put the fat into a large roasting pan, sprinkle generously with sea salt, and place in the preheated oven.

2 Meanwhile, cook the potatoes in a large saucepan of boiling water for 8–10 minutes, until parboiled. Drain well and cut the potatoes in half. Return the potatoes to the empty saucepan and shake vigorously to roughen their outsides.

3 Arrange the potatoes in a single layer in the hot fat and roast for 45 minutes. If they look as if they are beginning to char around the edges, reduce the oven temperature to 400°F. Turn the potatoes over and roast for an additional 30 minutes, until crisp. Serve garnished with rosemary sprigs.

FAMILY CELEBRATION DINNERS

MINI POPOVERS

Makes: 6   **Prep: 20 minutes**   **Cook: 35–40 minutes**

Ingredients

2 tablespoons beef dripping or sunflower oil

1 cup plus 2 tablespoons all-purpose flour

½ teaspoon salt

2 eggs

1 cup milk

Method

1 Grease six individual metal molds with the dripping, then divide the remaining dripping among the molds. Preheat the oven to 425°F, putting the molds into the oven so the dripping can melt while the oven heats.

2 Sift together the flour and salt into a large mixing bowl and make a well in the center. Break the eggs into the well, add the milk, and beat, gradually drawing in the flour from the side to make a smooth batter. Remove the molds from the oven and spoon in the batter until they are filled about halfway.

3 Bake in the preheated oven for 30–35 minutes, without opening the door, until the popovers are well risen, puffed, and golden brown. Serve immediately, because they will collapse if left to stand.

FAMILY CELEBRATION DINNERS

SEAFOOD GRATIN

Serves: 3-4   **Prep: 30-35 minutes**   **Cook: 25-30 minutes**

Ingredients

1½–1¾ pounds mussels

½ cup water

1 stick salted butter

2 onions, chopped

8 ounces shelled cockles or clams

juice and finely grated zest of ½ lemon

3 tablespoons chopped fresh parsley

2 cups coarse bread crumbs from a day-old ciabatta loaf

2 garlic cloves, finely chopped

salt and pepper

Method

1 Preheat the oven to 425°F. Scrub and debeard the mussels, discarding any with broken shells or that remain open. Put into a large saucepan with the water. Cover and steam for 4–5 minutes, until the shells open. Discard any that remain closed. Reserve eight mussels in their shells as a garnish. Remove the rest from the shells.

2 Melt half the butter in a skillet over medium–high heat. Add the onions and sauté for 7 minutes, until soft but not browned. Transfer to a 1¾-quart baking dish measuring about 10½ x 7½ inches.

3 Add the cockles, shelled mussels, lemon juice, and 2 tablespoons of the parsley. Season with salt and pepper and stir to mix.

4 Set aside a pat of butter and melt the remaining butter. Mix with the bread crumbs, garlic, lemon zest, and remaining parsley. Season with a little more salt and pepper. Spread the bread crumb mixture over the seafood. Top with the reserved mussels and dot them with the remaining butter.

5 Bake in the oven for 10–15 minutes, until the crumbs are golden and crisp and the seafood is thoroughly heated. Serve immediately.

ROASTED CAULIFLOWER, TOMATO & OLIVE GRATIN

Serves: 4　　　　**Prep: 30 minutes**　　　　**Cook: 1 hour 20 minutes**

Ingredients

4 tablespoons olive oil

2 tablespoons butter, plus extra for greasing

1 large onion, chopped

1½ teaspoons fresh thyme leaves

3 garlic cloves, thinly sliced

1 (28-ounce) can diced tomatoes

2–3 slivers lemon peel

2 cups coarse ciabatta bread crumbs

10–12 Kalamata olives, pitted and chopped

¼ cup chopped fresh flat-leaf parsley

1 large cauliflower

¼ cup coarsely grated vegetarian Parmesan-style cheese

sea salt and pepper

Method

1　Heat 2 tablespoons of the oil and half the butter in a deep skillet over medium heat. Add the onion and thyme and sauté for 5 minutes, until the onion is translucent. Add the garlic and sauté for 1–2 minutes, until just beginning to brown.

2　Stir in the tomatoes and lemon peel. Season with salt and pepper, then simmer, stirring, for 20 minutes, until thickened.

3　Preheat the oven to 400°F. Grease an ovenproof dish with butter. Combine the bread crumbs, olives, and parsley in a mixing bowl. Mix in the remaining oil.

4　Cut the cauliflower into quarters. Cut out the core. Break the florets into clumps and pack in a single layer in the prepared dish. Season with salt and pepper.

5　Pour in the tomato sauce, pushing it into the spaces between the florets. Sprinkle the bread crumb mixture evenly over the top. Dot with the remaining butter, then cover with aluminum foil.

6　Bake in the preheated oven for 35 minutes. Remove the foil and cook for another 15 minutes, until the cauliflower is tender-crisp and the crumbs are golden. Sprinkle with cheese and serve immediately.

CREAMED CHICKEN WITH JERUSALEM ARTICHOKES

Serves: 2   **Prep: 20 minutes**   **Cook: 30 minutes**

Ingredients

2 tablespoons butter

1 onion, finely chopped

1⅓ cups sliced Jerusalem artichokes

1 cup water

½ cup white wine

2 fresh tarragon sprigs or ½ teaspoon dried tarragon

2 skinless, boneless chicken breasts (about 4 ounces each)

1 teaspoon Dijon mustard

3 tablespoons crème fraîche or sour cream

salt and pepper

chopped fresh tarragon, to garnish (optional)

cooked rice, to serve

Method

1 Melt the butter in a large skillet over medium heat, add the onions, and sauté for 4–5 minutes, or until soft. Add the artichokes, water, wine, and tarragon. Bring to a boil, then reduce the heat and simmer, covered, for 5 minutes, or until the artichokes are just tender.

2 Cut each chicken breast into four pieces and add to the pan. Season with salt and pepper and continue to cook, stirring, for 10 minutes, or until the chicken is cooked through and shows no traces of pink.

3 Remove the tarragon sprigs and stir in the mustard and crème fraîche. Increase the heat and let the sauce simmer and thicken. Divide between two warm plates and garnish with chopped tarragon, if using. Serve immediately with cooked rice.

SLOW-ROASTED SHOULDER OF LAMB WITH HERB DUMPLINGS

Serves: 4–6   **Prep: 40–45 minutes**   **Cook: 4 hours**

Ingredients

2 large carrots,
cut into thin sticks

1 onion, sliced

3¼ pounds shoulder of lamb
on the bone

2–3 fresh bay leaves

1 sage sprig

small bunch parsley

2½ cups lamb or beef broth

salt and pepper

Herb-flavored dumplings

1 cup all-purpose flour

1 teaspoon baking powder

½ teaspoon salt

¼ teaspoon black pepper

1½ tablespoons finely
chopped
fresh parsley

1½ tablespoons finely
chopped fresh mint or
herb of your choice

2 tablespoons salted butter

1 egg

2 tablespoons milk

Method

1 Preheat the oven to 450°F. Spread out the carrots and onion in a roasting pan. Put the meat on top, tucking the herbs underneath. Season with salt and pepper, then pour in enough broth to almost cover the vegetables. Cover the pan with aluminum foil, sealing the edges. Roast for 20 minutes, then reduce the heat to 325°F and cook for another 3 hours.

2 For the dumplings, sift the flour, baking powder, and salt into a bowl. Mix in the pepper and herbs. Rub in the butter until the mixture resembles coarse bread crumbs. Beat the egg with the milk in a small bowl, then stir into the flour mixture to make a soft, slightly sticky dough. With floured hands, divide the dough into 12 pieces and roll into balls. Drop into a large saucepan of boiling salted water. Partly cover and cook for 15 minutes. Using tongs, gently lift the dumplings into a colander to drain for a few minutes. Transfer to a plate until needed.

3 Just before serving, heat the remaining broth in a saucepan. Remove the lamb from the oven and unseal the foil. Arrange the dumplings around the meat and pour in the broth. Reseal the foil; roast for 15 minutes. Transfer the lamb to a warm plate, discard the herbs, and put the dumplings and vegetables around the lamb. Strain the juices to serve with the lamb.

★ **Variation**

Add extra flavor with a generous splash of red wine to the broth in step 3.

PERFECT DESSERTS

DATE CAKE WITH CARAMEL SAUCE

Serves: 8

Prep: 25 minutes, plus soaking

Cook: 45–50 minutes

Ingredients

½ cup golden raisins

1 cup pitted and chopped dates

1 teaspoon baking soda

2 tablespoons butter, plus extra for greasing

1 cup firmly packed light brown sugar

2 eggs

1⅔ cups all-purpose flour, sifted with 1½ teaspoons baking powder

Caramel sauce

2 tablespoons butter

¾ cup heavy cream

1 cup firmly packed light brown sugar, sifted

Method

1 Preheat the oven to 350°F. Grease an 8-inch round cake pan. To make the cake, put the golden raisins, dates, and baking soda into a heatproof bowl. Cover with boiling water and let soak. Put the butter into a separate bowl, add the sugar, and mix well.

2 Beat the eggs into the butter mixture, then fold in the flour mixture. Drain the soaked fruit, add to the bowl, and mix. Spoon the batter evenly into the prepared cake pan. Bake in the preheated oven for 35–40 minutes, or until a toothpick inserted into the center comes out clean.

3 About 5 minutes before the end of the cooking time, make the sauce. Melt the butter in a saucepan over medium heat. Stir in the cream and sugar and bring to a boil, stirring constantly. Reduce the heat and simmer for 5 minutes. Cut the pudding into equal portions, pour the sauce over the slices, and serve immediately.

★ **Variation**

For a twist on this classic dessert, when making the sauce, stir in 2 tablespoons of black coffee for an irresistible taste.

LEMON MERINGUE PIE

Serves: 8

Prep: 40 minutes, **Cook: 1 hour**
plus chilling and cooling

Ingredients

Pastry dough

1¼ cups all-purpose flour, plus extra for dusting

6 tablespoons butter, cut into small pieces, plus extra for greasing

¼ cup confectioners' sugar, sifted

finely grated zest of ½ lemon

½ egg yolk, beaten

1½ tablespoons milk

Filling

3 tablespoons cornstarch

1¼ cups water

juice and grated zest of 2 lemons

¾ cup plus 2 tablespoons superfine or granulated sugar

2 eggs, separated

Method

1 To make the dough, sift the flour into a bowl. Rub in the butter with your fingertips until the mixture resembles fine bread crumbs. Mix in the remaining dough ingredients. Turn out onto a lightly floured work surface and knead briefly. Roll into a ball, wrap in plastic wrap, and chill in the refrigerator for 30 minutes.

2 Preheat the oven to 350°F. Grease an 8-inch round tart pan. Roll out the dough to a thickness of ¼ inch, then use it to line the bottom and side of the pan. Prick all over with a fork, line with parchment paper, and fill with pie weights or dried beans. Bake in the preheated oven for 15 minutes. Remove the pastry shell from the oven and take out the paper and weights. Reduce the oven temperature to 300°F.

3 To make the filling, mix the cornstarch with a little of the water to form a paste. Put the remaining water in a saucepan. Stir in the lemon juice, lemon zest, and cornstarch paste. Bring to a boil, stirring. Cook for 2 minutes. Let cool slightly. Stir in ⅓ cup of the superfine sugar and the egg yolks, then pour into the pastry shell.

4 Whisk the egg whites in a clean bowl until stiff. Gradually whisk in the remaining superfine sugar and spread the meringue over the pie. Bake for an additional 40 minutes. Remove from the oven, cool, and serve.

PERFECT DESSERTS

GOLDEN SHOOFLY PIE

Serves: 8

Prep: 30 minutes,
plus chilling and cooling

Cook: 35–40 minutes

Ingredients

1 sheet ready-to-bake rolled dough pie crust

all-purpose flour, for dusting

1½ cups light corn syrup

3 cups fresh white bread crumbs

½ cup heavy cream

finely grated zest of ½ lemon or orange

2 tablespoons lemon juice or orange juice

whipped cream or ice cream, to serve

Method

1 Roll out the dough on a lightly floured work surface and use to line an 8-inch tart pan, reserving the pastry scraps. Prick the bottom of the pastry shell all over with a fork, cover with plastic wrap, and chill in the refrigerator for 30 minutes. Reroll the reserved dough scraps and cut out small shapes, such as leaves, stars, or hearts, to decorate the top of the tart.

2 Preheat the oven to 375°F. Mix the corn syrup, bread crumbs, heavy cream, and lemon zest with the lemon juice in a small bowl.

3 Pour the filling into the pastry shell and decorate the top of the pie with the dough shapes of your choice. Transfer to the preheated oven and bake for 35–40 minutes, or until the filling is just set.

4 Let the pie cool slightly before serving. Cut into wedges and serve with a dollop of whipped cream or ice cream.

APPLE & MIXED BERRY CRISP

Serves: 6   **Prep: 25 minutes**   **Cook: 50–55 minutes**

Ingredients

2 large cooking apples, such as Granny Smiths (about 1 pound), peeled and cut into bite-size chunks

1 cup blackberries

¼ cup elderberries, black currants, or blueberries

⅓ cup firmly packed brown sugar

½ teaspoon ground cinnamon

1 tablespoon water

Crumb topping

1⅓ cups all-purpose flour

¼ cup rolled oats

6 tablespoons butter, diced

⅓ cup firmly packed brown sugar

½ cup chopped hazelnuts

Method

1 Preheat the oven to 375°F. Put the apples, blackberries, and elderberries into a 1¼-quart baking dish. Stir in the sugar, cinnamon, and water. Cover tightly with aluminum foil and bake in the preheated oven for 30 minutes, until the apples are softened but not cooked right through.

2 For the crumb topping, mix the flour and oats together in a bowl. Add the butter and rub in with your fingertips until the mixture resembles fine bread crumbs. Stir in the sugar and hazelnuts.

3 Remove the foil from the baked fruit and stir. Sprinkle the mixture evenly over the top. Return to the oven for 20–25 minutes, until lightly browned and starting to bubble at the edges. Serve immediately.

1

3

IRISH WHISKEY TRIFLE

Serves: 8

Prep: 35–40 minutes, plus cooling, soaking, and chilling

Cook: 10 minutes

Ingredients

10 ladyfingers
or 1 stale sponge cake

raspberry preserves,
for spreading

2 macarons,
lightly crushed

finely grated zest of 1 lemon

2 tablespoons Irish whiskey

½ cup sherry

1¼ cups heavy cream

½ tablespoons sugar

1¼ cups raspberries

candied violets or miniature
macarons, to decorate

Custard

5 egg yolks, lightly beaten

¼ cup sugar

2 teaspoons cornstarch

½ cup milk

1 cup heavy cream

½ teaspoon vanilla extract

Method

1 First make the custard. Combine the egg yolks and sugar in a mixing bowl. Stir in the cornstarch and mix to a smooth paste, then whisk in the milk.

2 Heat the cream in a heavy saucepan until just starting to simmer but not boiling. Gradually whisk the hot cream into the egg mixture, then return the mixture to the pan. Whisk constantly over medium heat for about 5 minutes, until thickened. Immediately pour into a small bowl and stir in the vanilla extract. Cover with plastic wrap to prevent a skin from forming and let cool completely.

3 Thickly spread half of the ladyfingers with raspberry preserves. Place the remaining ladyfingers on top to make a sandwich. If using sponge cake, slice horizontally into two or three layers and spread with preserves. Arrange in a single layer in the bottom of a deep serving dish. Sprinkle with the crushed macarons and the lemon zest.

4 Combine the whiskey and sherry and pour over the ladyfinger mixture. Let soak for 1 hour.

5 Spoon the cooled custard over the ladyfinger mixture.

6 Whip the cream with the sugar until stiff peaks form. Spread over the custard, leveling with a spatula. Cover with plastic wrap and chill for 1 hour, or until ready to serve.

7 Arrange the raspberries on top and decorate with candied violets or miniature macarons.

CHOCOLATE PUDDING

Serves: 6

Prep: 20-25 minutes, plus optional cooling and chilling

Cook: 10-15 minutes

Ingredients

½ cup sugar

¼ cup unsweetened cocoa powder

2 tablespoons cornstarch

pinch of salt

1½ cups milk

1 egg, beaten

4 tablespoons butter

½ teaspoon vanilla extract

heavy cream, to serve (optional)

Method

1 Put the sugar, cocoa powder, cornstarch, and salt into a heatproof bowl. Stir and set aside.

2 Pour the milk into a saucepan and heat over medium heat until just simmering. Do not bring to a boil.

3 Keeping the pan over medium heat, spoon a little of the simmering milk into the sugar mixture and blend, then stir this mixture into the milk in the pan. Beat in the egg and half of the butter and reduce the heat to low.

4 Simmer for 5–8 minutes, stirring frequently, until the mixture thickens. Remove from the heat and add the vanilla extract and the remaining butter, stirring until the butter melts and is absorbed.

5 The pudding can be served hot or chilled, with cream for pouring over the top, if desired. If chilling the pudding, spoon it into a serving bowl, press plastic wrap onto the surface to prevent a skin from forming, let cool, then chill in the refrigerator until required.

PERFECT DESSERTS

LEMON & LIME EGG-FREE CUSTARD

Serves: 4

Prep: 20 minutes,
plus cooling and chilling

Cook: 8 minutes

Ingredients

2 cups heavy cream

¾ cup superfine or granulated sugar

finely grated zest and juice of 1 large lemon

finely grated zest and juice of 1 lime, plus extra zest to serve

1⅓ cups hulled and halved strawberries

shortbread cookies, to serve (optional)

Method

1 Put the cream and sugar into a saucepan. Bring slowly to a boil and simmer for 3 minutes, stirring occasionally.

2 Remove from the heat, add the lemon and lime zests and juices and whisk well. Pour into four glasses, let cool, then cover and place in the refrigerator for 2–3 hours, until set and well chilled.

3 Divide the strawberries and extra lime zest among the glasses and serve with shortbread cookies, if desired.

PERFECT DESSERTS

SPONGE CAKE IN SYRUP WITH CUSTARD

Serves: 4　　　**Prep: 20 minutes**　　　**Cook: 4 minutes,**
plus standing

Ingredients

¼ cup light corn syrup

1 stick butter, plus extra for greasing

⅓ cup superfine or granulated sugar

2 eggs, lightly beaten

1 cup all-purpose flour

2 teaspoons baking powder

about 2 tablespoons warm water

prepared custard, vanilla pudding, or ice cream to serve

Method

1 Grease a deep 1½-quart microwave-safe bowl with butter. Spoon the light corn syrup into the prepared bowl.

2 Beat the butter with the sugar in a bowl until pale and fluffy. Gradually add the eggs, beating well after each addition.

3 Sift together the flour and baking powder, then gently fold the flour mixture into the butter mixture. Add enough water to create a soft, dropping consistency. Spoon the batter into the bowl and level the surface.

4 Cover with microwave-safe plastic wrap, leaving a small space to let the air escape. Cook in a microwave oven on high for 4 minutes, then remove and let the pudding stand for 5 minutes while it continues to cook.

5 Turn out the dessert onto a serving plate. Serve immediately with custard, vanilla pudding, or ice cream.

RHUBARB CRISP

Serves: 6 **Prep: 25 minutes** **Cook: 25–30 minutes**

Ingredients

18 rhubarb stalks
(about 2 pounds)

⅔ cup sugar

grated zest and juice of
1 orange

cream, ice cream, or
custard, to serve

Crumb topping

1¾ cups all-purpose flour or
whole wheat flour

1 stick unsalted butter

½ cup firmly packed light
brown sugar

1 teaspoon ground ginger

Method

1 Preheat the oven to 375°F.

2 Cut the rhubarb into 1-inch lengths and put into
a 1¾-quart ovenproof dish with the sugar and
the orange zest and juice.

3 Make the crumb topping by putting the flour into
a mixing bowl and rubbing in the butter until the
mixture resembles bread crumbs. Stir in the sugar
and the ginger.

4 Spread the crumb topping evenly over the fruit
and press down lightly using a fork. Bake in the
center of the preheated oven on a baking sheet
for 25–30 minutes, until the topping is golden
brown. Serve with cream.

STRAWBERRY ICE CREAM SUNDAE

Serves: 4   **Prep: 20–25 minutes**   **Cook: no cooking**

Ingredients

1 pound strawberries, hulled

2 tablespoons confectioners' sugar

1 tablespoon lemon juice

⅔ cup heavy cream

2 cups vanilla ice cream

¼ cup blanched almonds, toasted and chopped

Method

1 Put a generous 1 cup of the strawberries into a mixing bowl with the sugar and lemon juice and puree with an electric handheld blender until smooth.

2 Rub the puree through a fine strainer into a bowl, and discard the seeds.

3 Whip the cream until thick enough to hold soft peaks. Slice the remaining strawberries. Layer the strawberries, scoops of ice cream, and spoonfuls of whipped cream in four glasses.

4 Spoon the puree over the sundaes and sprinkle with chopped almonds. Serve immediately.

WHISKEY FUDGE

Makes: 16

Prep: 25–30 minutes, plus **Cook: 20–25 minutes**
cooling, chilling, and storing

Ingredients

a little sunflower oil,
for greasing

1¼ cups firmly packed light
brown sugar

1 stick unsalted butter,
diced

1 (14-ounce) can
sweetened condensed milk

2 tablespoons
light corn syrup

6 ounces semisweet
chocolate, coarsely
chopped

¼ cup Irish whiskey

¼ cup walnut pieces

Method

1 Lightly brush an 8-inch square baking pan with oil. Line it with nonstick parchment paper, snipping diagonally into the corners, then pressing the paper into the pan so that the bottom and sides are lined. Put the sugar, butter, condensed milk, and corn syrup into a heavy saucepan. Heat gently, stirring, until the sugar has dissolved.

2 Increase the heat and boil for 12–15 minutes, or until the mixture reaches 240°F on a candy thermometer. (Alternatively, spoon a little of the syrup into some iced water; it will form a soft ball when it is ready.) As the temperature rises, stir the fudge occasionally so the sugar doesn't stick and burn. Remove the fudge from the heat. Add the chocolate and whiskey and stir together until the chocolate has melted and the mixture is smooth.

3 Preheat the broiler to medium–hot. Put the walnuts on a baking sheet and toast them under the broiler for 2–3 minutes, or until browned, then coarsely chop them. Pour the mixture into the prepared baking pan, smooth the surface using a spatula, and sprinkle with the walnuts. Let cool for 1 hour. Cover with plastic wrap, then chill in the refrigerator for 1–2 hours, or until firm. Lift the fudge out of the pan, peel off the paper, and cut into small squares. Store in an airtight container in a cool, dry place for up to two weeks.

PERFECT DESSERTS

PEANUT BRITTLE

**Makes: about
1 pound**

Prep: 25 minutes,
plus cooling

Cook: 15 minutes

Ingredients

vegetable or sunflower oil,
for oiling

1 cup granulated sugar

⅓ cup firmly packed light
brown sugar

⅓ cup light corn syrup

2 tablespoons butter

⅓ cup water

1 cup coarsely chopped
salted peanuts

1 teaspoon vanilla extract

¼ teaspoon baking soda

Method

1 Preheat the oven to 250°F. Line a 12-inch square baking pan with aluminum foil and oil lightly. Place in the preheated oven to warm.

2 Meanwhile, put the sugars, light corn syrup, butter, and water into a heavy saucepan. Heat gently, stirring, until the butter has melted and the sugar has completely dissolved.

3 Brush around the inside of the pan above the level of the syrup, using a pastry brush dipped in water, then turn up the heat and boil rapidly until the syrup reaches 300°F on a candy thermometer. (Alternatively, drop a spoonful into a glass of cold water; if ready, it should form into threads).

4 Working quickly, remove from the heat and stir in the peanuts, followed by the vanilla extract and baking soda. Pour onto the warm baking sheet and tilt gently to level the surface. Let stand for about 30 minutes to cool, then snap into pieces. Store in airtight bags or containers.

PERFECT DESSERTS

PEPPERMINT CREAMS

Makes: 25

Prep: 25–30 minutes, plus chilling, setting, and storing

Cook: 5 minutes

Ingredients

1 extra-large egg white

cups confectioners' sugar, ﬁed, plus extra for dipping, if needed

a few drops of peppermint extract

a few drops of green food coloring

4 ounces semisweet colate, coarsely chopped

Method

1 Line a baking sheet with a sheet of nonstick parchment paper.

2 Lightly whisk the egg white in a large, clean mixing bowl until it is frothy but still translucent.

3 Add the sifted confectioners' sugar to the egg white and stir, using a wooden spoon, until the mixture is stiff. Knead in the peppermint extract and food coloring.

4 Using the palms of your hands, roll the mixture into walnut-size balls and place them on the prepared baking sheet. Use a fork to flatten them; if it sticks to them, dip it in confectioners' sugar before pressing. Put the creams into the refrigerator to set for 24 hours.

5 Put the chocolate into a heatproof bowl, set the bowl over a saucepan of gently simmering water, and heat until melted. Dip the creams halfway into the chocolate and return to the baking sheet for 1 hour, or until set. Store in an airtight container in the refrigerator for up to 5 days.

PERFECT DESSERTS

NUT FUDGE

Makes: 80

Prep: 25 minutes,
plus cooling

Cook: 20 minutes

Ingredients

1¼ cups milk

5 cups granulated sugar

2 sticks butter,
plus extra for greasing

2 tablespoons
instant coffee

2 tablespoons
unsweetened cocoa
powder

2 tablespoons
light corn syrup

1 (14-ounce) can
sweetened condensed milk

1 cup chopped pecans

Method

1 Grease a 12 x 9-inch baking pan. Put the milk, sugar, and butter into a large saucepan. Stir over a gentle heat until the sugar has dissolved. Stir in the coffee, cocoa, light corn syrup, and condensed milk.

2 Bring to a boil and boil steadily, whisking constantly, for 10 minutes, or until a little of the mixture dropped into a small bowl of cold water forms a soft ball when rolled between the fingers.

3 Cool for 5 minutes, then beat vigorously with a wooden spoon until the mixture starts to thicken. Stir in the nuts. Continue beating until the mixture becomes thick, creamy, and grainy. Quickly pour into the prepared pan and let stand in a cool place to set. Cut the fudge into squares to serve.

PERFECT DESSERTS

COCONUT ICE

Makes: 50

Prep: 25–30 minutes,   Cook: No cooking
plus setting

Ingredients

oil, for greasing

1 (14-ounce) can
veetened condensed milk

1 teaspoon vanilla extract

4 cups dry unsweetened
coconut

2⅓ cups confectioners'
sugar

3 tablespoons
unsweetened cocoa
powder, sifted

few drops of red or pink
food coloring (optional)

Method

1 Grease the bottom of a shallow 7-inch square cake pan and line with parchment paper. Mix the condensed milk and vanilla extract together in a large bowl. Add the coconut and confectioners' sugar. Mix together with a wooden spoon until the mixture becomes stiff.

2 Transfer half of the mixture to another bowl. Add the cocoa powder and mix well until it is an even color. Spread over the bottom of the prepared pan and press down with the back of a spoon.

3 If using food coloring, mix a few drops into the remaining bowl of mixture until evenly pink. Spread the pink mixture over the chocolate layer and smooth the top. Let set overnight before turning out and cutting into squares.

PERFECT DESSERTS

IRISH BUTTERMILK PANCAKES

Makes: 12

Prep: 25 minutes, plus standing

Cook: 15–20 minutes

Ingredients

1⅓ cups all-purpose flour

2 teaspoons sugar

½ teaspoon salt

1 teaspoon baking soda

1 egg, lightly beaten

1½ cups buttermilk

3 tablespoons vegetable oil, plus extra for brushing

To serve

⅔ cup heavy cream, whipped

1 cup blueberries

Method

1 Sift the flour, sugar, salt, and baking soda into a medium mixing bowl.

2 Mix the egg with the buttermilk and vegetable oil in a small mixing bowl. Add to the dry ingredients, beating to a smooth, creamy batter. Let stand for at least 30 minutes or up to 2 hours.

3 Heat a nonstick pancake pan or skillet over medium heat and brush with vegetable oil. Pour in enough batter to make 4-inch circles (about ¼ cup per pancake). Cook for 1½–2 minutes per side, or until small bubbles appear on the surface. Transfer to a dish and keep warm while you cook the rest.

4 Serve with whipped cream and blueberries.

CHOCOLATE & STOUT ICE CREAM

Makes: about 3½ cups

Prep: 35–40 minutes, plus cooling, chilling, and freezing

Cook: 25 minutes

Ingredients

1½ cups milk

¾ cup sugar

6 ounces bittersweet chocolate, broken into small pieces

4 egg yolks

1 teaspoon vanilla extract

1⅓ cups stout

1 cup heavy cream

grated chocolate, to decorate

Method

1 Pour the milk into a saucepan and add the sugar. Bring to a boil, stirring, until the sugar has dissolved. Remove from the heat and stir in the chocolate.

2 Pour the egg yolks into a heatproof bowl and beat for 5 minutes, or until the whisk or beaters leave a faint trail when lifted from the mixture. Stir some of the warm chocolate mixture into the egg yolks, then gradually beat in the rest.

3 Place the bowl over a saucepan of gently boiling water. Stir constantly for about 10 minutes, until the mixture reaches a temperature of 185°F, or is thick enough to coat the back of a spoon. Be careful to not let it boil.

4 Strain the mixture through a fine strainer into a small bowl. Stir in the vanilla extract. Sit the bottom of the small bowl in iced water until cold, then cover with plastic wrap and chill for 2 hours.

5 Meanwhile, pour the stout into a saucepan and bring to a boil. Reduce the heat and simmer briskly for 8 minutes, until reduced to 1 cup. Pour into a small bowl, let cool, then chill in the refrigerator.

6 Stir the cream and chilled stout into the chocolate mixture, mixing well, then pour the mixture into the bowl of an ice cream machine.

7 Churn the mixture and then freeze it, following the manufacturer's directions. Alternatively, pour the mixture into a shallow, freezer-proof container, cover with plastic wrap, and freeze for about 2 hours, until beginning to harden around the edges. Beat until smooth to get rid of any ice crystals. Freeze again and repeat the process two times, then freeze until completely firm.

8 Move the ice cream to the refrigerator 30 minutes before serving to soften. Serve in chilled dishes, sprinkled with grated chocolate.

CREAM PUFFS WITH CHOCOLATE & BRANDY SAUCE

Serves: 4

Prep: 40–45 minutes,   Cook: 35 minutes
plus cooling

Ingredients

Choux pastry dough

5 tablespoons unsalted butter, plus extra for greasing

1 cup water

¾ cup all-purpose flour

3 eggs, beaten

Cream filling

1¼ cups heavy cream

3 tablespoons sugar

1 teaspoon vanilla extract

Chocolate and brandy sauce

4 ounces semisweet chocolate, broken into small pieces

2½ tablespoons unsalted butter

⅓ cup water

2 tablespoons brandy

Method

1 Preheat the oven to 400°F. Grease several large baking sheets.

2 To make the dough, put the butter and water into a saucepan and bring to a boil. Meanwhile, sift the flour into a bowl. Turn off the heat and beat in the flour until smooth. Cool for 5 minutes. Beat in enough of the eggs to give the mixture a soft, dropping consistency.

3 Transfer to a pastry bag fitted with a ½ -inch plain tip. Pipe small balls onto the prepared baking sheets. Bake in the preheated oven for 25 minutes. Remove from the oven. Pierce each ball with the tip of a sharp knife to let the steam escape.

4 To make the filling, whip the cream, sugar, and vanilla extract together. Cut the pastry balls across the middle, then fill with the cream.

5 To make the sauce, gently melt the chocolate, butter, and water together in a small saucepan, stirring constantly, until smooth. Stir in the brandy.

6 Pile the profiteroles into individual serving dishes, pour the sauce over them, and serve.

CHOCOLATE ORANGE TART

Serves: 6

Prep: 35 minutes,
plus chilling and cooling

Cook: 40–50 minutes

Ingredients

1 sheet ready-to-bake rolled dough pie crust

4 ounces bittersweet chocolate, broken into pieces

4 tablespoons butter, cut into pieces

⅓ cup firmly packed light brown sugar

2 extra-large eggs

finely grated zest of 1 large orange

¼ cup all-purpose flour, plus extra for dusting

3 tablespoons orange juice

2 clementines, peeled and thinly sliced (optional), and unsweetened cocoa powder, to decorate

crème fraîche or whipped cream, to serve

Method

1 Thinly roll out the dough on a lightly floured surface and use to line an 8½-inch tart pan. Chill for 20 minutes.

2 Meanwhile, preheat the oven to 400°F. Line the pastry shell with parchment paper and fill with pie weights or dried beans. Bake in the preheated oven for 15 minutes, then remove the weights and paper and return to the oven for an additional 5–10 minutes, until the bottom is crisp.

3 Put the chocolate and butter into a heatproof bowl set over a saucepan of gently simmering water and heat, stirring occasionally, until melted and smooth. Put the sugar, eggs, and orange zest into a separate bowl and whisk together until frothy and the sugar has dissolved completely. Sift the flour over the top. Add the melted chocolate mixture and the orange juice and stir together until completely smooth.

4 Pour into the pastry shell and return to the oven for 15–20 minutes, until the filling is just set in the middle. Cool for at least 30 minutes, then remove from the pan. Serve warm or chill overnight; the filling will become dense and trufflelike. To serve, sift a little cocoa powder over the top of the tart and decorate with sliced clementines, if using. Serve with crème fraîche or whipped cream.

MIXED FRUIT & BREAD DESSERT

Serves: 6   **Prep: 35 minutes,** plus chilling   **Cook: 3–4 minutes**

Ingredients

5 cups mixed blueberries, raspberries, and/or red or black currants plus extra to decorate (optional)

3–4 tablespoons sugar

⅓ cup port

2 cups strawberries, hulled and halved or quartered if large

6–7 slices thick white bread, crusts removed

heavy cream, to serve

Method

1 Remove the currants, if using, from their stems and put into a saucepan with the rest of the fruit (except the strawberries), 2 tablespoons of the sugar, and half the port. Simmer gently for 3–4 minutes, until the fruits start to release their juices. Remove from the heat. Add the strawberries and stir in the remaining sugar to taste.

2 Line a deep, round 1-quart ovenproof dish with plastic wrap, letting the ends overhang. Put the fruits into a strainer set over a bowl to catch the juices, then stir the remaining port into the juices. Cut a circle the same size as the bottom of the bowl out of one slice of bread. Dip in the juice mixture to coat and place in the bottom of the bowl.

3 Reserve one slice of bread. Cut the rest in half slightly on an angle. Dip the pieces, one at a time, in the juice mixture and place around the sides of the bowl, narrowest end down, pushing them together so there aren't any gaps and trimming the final piece of bread to fit (as well as any other pieces that are overhanging and need trimming).

4 Fill with the fruit, then cover with the reserved piece of bread, cut to fit the top of the bowl. Put a small plate on top and weigh it down with a can or two. Some juices may escape, so put the bowl onto a plate to catch any spills. Chill overnight in the refrigerator. Set aside any remaining juice in the refrigerator.

5 Remove the weight and plate, then cover the dessert with a plate and flip over. Remove the bowl and plastic wrap and decorate with extra fruits (if using). Serve with any remaining juice and cream.

IRISH CREAM CHEESECAKE

Serves: 8

Prep: 30 minutes, **Cook: 10 minutes**
plus chilling and cooling

Ingredients

vegetable oil, for oiling

18 chocolate chip cookies
(about 6 ounces)

4 tablespoons unsalted
butter

crème fraîche or
whipped cream and fresh
strawberries, to serve

Filling

8 ounces semisweet
chocolate, broken into
pieces

8 ounces milk chocolate,
broken into pieces

¼ cup sugar

1½ cups cream cheese

2 cups heavy cream,
lightly whipped

3 tablespoons Irish Cream
liqueur

Method

1 Line the bottom of an 8-inch round springform cake pan with parchment paper and brush the sides with oil. Put the cookies into a plastic bag and crush with a rolling pin. Put the butter into a saucepan and heat gently until melted. Stir in the crushed cookies. Press into the bottom of the prepared cake pan and chill in the refrigerator for 1 hour.

2 To make the filling, put the semisweet and milk chocolates into a heatproof bowl set over a saucepan of gently simmering water until melted. Let cool. Put the sugar and cream cheese into a bowl and beat together until smooth, then fold in the lightly whipped cream. Fold the melted chocolate into the cream cheese mixture, then stir in the liqueur.

3 Spoon into the cake pan and smooth the surface. Let chill in the refrigerator for 2 hours, or until firm. Transfer to a serving plate and cut into slices. Serve with crème fraîche and strawberries.

CHOCOLATE BREAD PUDDING

Serves: 4

Prep: 30 minutes,
plus chilling and standing

Cook: 45–50 minutes

Ingredients

6 slices thick white bread, crusts removed

2 cups milk

¾ cup canned evaporated milk

2 tablespoons unsweetened cocoa powder

2 eggs

2 tablespoons packed light brown sugar

1 teaspoon vanilla extract

confectioners' sugar, for dusting

Hot fudge sauce

2 ounces semisweet chocolate, broken into pieces

1 tablespoon unsweetened cocoa powder

2 tablespoons light corn syrup

4 tablespoons butter, plus extra for greasing

2 tablespoons packed light brown sugar

⅔ cup milk

1 tablespoon cornstarch

Method

1 Grease a shallow, ovenproof baking dish. Cut the bread into squares and layer them in the dish.

2 Put the milk, evaporated milk, and cocoa powder into a saucepan and heat gently, stirring occasionally, until the mixture is lukewarm. Whisk together the eggs, sugar, and vanilla extract in a small bowl. Add the warm milk mixture and beat together well.

3 Pour into the prepared dish, making sure that all the bread is completely covered. Cover the dish with plastic wrap and chill in the refrigerator for 1–2 hours, then bake in a preheated oven, 350°F, for 35–40 minutes, until set. Let stand for 5 minutes.

4 To make the sauce, put all the ingredients into a saucepan and heat gently, stirring constantly, until smooth.

5 Dust the chocolate bread pudding with confectioners' sugar and serve immediately with the hot fudge sauce.

GOOSEBERRY WHIP

Serves: 4

Prep: 25 minutes, **Cook: 15 minutes**
plus cooling and chilling

Ingredients

2 cups fresh gooseberries, trimmed, or 1⅓ cups canned gooseberries, drained

¼ cup sugar

finely grated zest of 1 lime

1 tablespoon water

1 cup heavy cream

½ cup elderflower syrup

shortbread cookies and lime zest, to serve

Method

1 Put the gooseberries into a saucepan with the sugar, lime zest, and water. Heat until simmering then cover and cook for 10 minutes, until the fruit bursts.

2 Transfer to a bowl and crush the fruit against the side of the bowl with a fork. Let cool completely, then chill for 20 minutes.

3 Whisk the cream and elderflower syrup together with a handheld electric mixer until the mixture holds its shape, then fold in the gooseberries. Spoon into four small glasses. Serve chilled with the cookies and decorated with lime zest.

PERFECT DESSERTS

CHOCOLATE & BANANA SUNDAE

Serves: 4　　　　**Prep: 30 minutes**　　　　**Cook: 5 minutes**

Ingredients

Chocolate sauce

2 ounce semisweet chocolate

¼ cup light corn syrup

1 tablespoons butter

1 tablespoon brandy or dark rum (optional)

Sundae

⅔ cup heavy cream

4 bananas, peeled

8 scoops vanilla ice cream

½ cup mixed nuts, toasted and chopped

2 ounces milk or semisweet chocolate, grated

4 thin cookies, to serve (optional)

Method

1 To make the chocolate sauce, break the chocolate into small pieces and put into a heatproof bowl with the light corn syrup and butter. Set over a saucepan of gently simmering water, stirring, until melted and well combined. Remove the bowl from the heat and stir in the brandy, if using.

2 To make the sundae, whip the cream until just holding its shape and slice the bananas. Place a scoop of ice cream in the bottom of each of four tall sundae glasses. Top with slices of banana, some chocolate sauce, a spoonful of cream, and a generous sprinkling of nuts.

3 Repeat the layers, finishing with a good dollop of cream, then sprinkle with the remaining nuts and the grated chocolate. Serve with thin cookies, if desired.

KNICKERBOCKER GLORY

Serves: 4

Prep: 30 minutes,
plus cooling

Cook: 7–10 minutes

Ingredients

Melba sauce

1½ cups raspberries

1½ tablespoons confectioners' sugar, sifted

Chocolate sauce

2 ounces semisweet chocolate, chopped

1 tablespoon packed light brown sugar

½ cup milk

Filling

2 cups fresh fruit (such as sliced banana, halved seedless grapes, hulled and halved strawberries, pineapple chunks, chopped nectarines, and/or raspberries)

8 small scoops vanilla ice cream

Topping

1 cup heavy cream, whipped

¼ cup mixed nuts, toasted and chopped

4 thin cookies (optional)

4 pitted fresh cherries or maraschino cherries

Method

1 To make the Melba sauce, place the raspberries and confectioners' sugar into a food processor and blend to a puree. Rub through a strainer and discard the seeds.

2 To make the chocolate sauce, put all the ingredients into a small, heavy saucepan and heat gently until melted. Stir well and simmer for 2 minutes. Cool.

3 Assemble the Knickerbocker Glory just before serving. Spoon alternate layers of fruit, ice cream, and Melba sauce into four tall sundae glasses, filling them almost to the top.

4 Top each glass with a spoonful of cream, then drizzle with the chocolate sauce and sprinkle nuts on top. Add a thin cookie to each glass, if using, and finish with a cherry. Serve immediately

MERINGUE & MIXED BERRY DESSERT

Serves: 6

Prep: 30–35 minutes,   Cook: 55–60 minutes
plus cooling

Ingredients

2½ cups milk

2 tablespoons butter,
plus extra for greasing

finely grated zest of 1 lemon

¾ cup sugar

2 cups fresh
white bread crumbs

4 extra-large eggs,
separated

3 tablespoons raspberry
preserves or jam, warmed

1 cup blueberries

1 cup raspberries

light cream, to serve

Method

1 Put the milk, butter, and lemon zest into a saucepan. Heat to simmering point then add 2 tablespoons of the sugar and stir to dissolve. Remove from the heat and stir in the bread crumbs. Let cool and soften for 20 minutes.

2 Preheat the oven to 325°F. Whisk the egg yolks into the bread crumb mixture and pour into a lightly greased 1¼-quart baking dish. Bake in the preheated oven for 40 minutes or until just set in the middle. Keep the oven on.

3 Spread the preserves over the top of the dessert, being careful not to break the surface too much. Mix the blueberries and raspberries together and sprinkle over the top.

4 Place the egg whites in a clean bowl and whisk with an electric mixer until forming stiff peaks. Slowly beat in the remaining sugar, one tablespoon at a time, until the meringue is thick and glossy. Spoon the meringue over the dessert, covering the top completely, and return to the oven for 10–15 minutes, until just browned. Serve immediately with cream.

BLACKBERRY SOUP WITH BUTTERMILK CUSTARDS

Serves: 4

Prep: 30 minutes, plus soaking, chilling, and cooling

Cook: 15 minutes

Ingredients

Buttermilk custards

4 sheets gelatin

1 cup plus 2 tablespoons buttermilk

1 cup plus 2 tablespoons heavy cream

¼ cup milk

½ cup sugar

Blackberry soup

3 cups blackberries (about 1 pound)

1¼ cups fruity red wine

½ cup water

⅓ cup sugar, or to taste

2 star anise

¼–⅓ cup blackberry liqueur (optional)

Method

1 To make the custards, put the gelatin into a small bowl, cover with cold water, and let soak for 5 minutes. Meanwhile, heat the buttermilk, cream, and milk together in a saucepan to just below boiling point. Add the sugar and stir until it has completely dissolved. Remove the gelatin from the soaking liquid and squeeze out any excess water. Add to the hot buttermilk mixture and stir until completely dissolved. Pour through a fine strainer and fill four dariole molds or individual dessert molds. Transfer to the refrigerator and chill for several hours, or overnight, until set.

2 To make the blackberry soup, put the blackberries, wine, and water into a large saucepan with the sugar and star anise. Simmer gently for 8–10 minutes, until the sugar has dissolved and the mixture has a lovely anise scent. Remove from the heat and let cool. Once the mixture has cooled, remove and discard the star anise, transfer the mixture to a food processor, and blend until smooth. Pour through a fine strainer and stir in the liqueur, if using. Cover and chill in the refrigerator until ready to serve.

3 To serve, divide the blackberry soup among four soup plates (not deep bowls) and place a buttermilk custard in the center of each.

LATTICED CHERRY PIE

Serves: 8   **Prep: 40 minutes, plus chilling**   **Cook: 55 minutes**

Ingredients

Pastry dough

1 cup plus 2 tablespoons all-purpose flour, plus extra for dusting

¼ teaspoon baking powder

½ teaspoon allspice

½ teaspoon salt

¼ cup sugar

4 tablespoons unsalted butter, chilled and diced, plus extra for greasing

1 egg, beaten, plus extra for glazing

Filling

4 cups pitted fresh cherries, or 2 (15-ounce) cans cherries, drained

¾ cup sugar

½ teaspoon almond extract

2 teaspoon cherry brandy

¼ teaspoon allspice

2 tablespoons cornstarch

2 tablespoons water

2 tablespoons unsalted butter, melted

ice cream, to serve

Method

1 To make the dough, sift the flour with the baking powder into a large bowl. Stir in the allspice, salt, and sugar. Rub in the butter until the mixture resembles fine bread crumbs, make a well in the center, pour in the egg, and mix into a dough. Cut the dough in half, and use your hands to roll each half into a ball. Wrap in plastic wrap and chill in the refrigerator for 30 minutes. Preheat the oven to 425°F. Grease a 9-inch pie plate. Roll out the dough balls into two circles, each 12 inches in diameter. Use one to line the pie plate.

2 To make the filling, put half the cherries and all the sugar into a saucepan. Bring to a simmer and stir in the almond extract, brandy, and allspice. In a bowl, mix the cornstarch and water into a paste. Stir the paste into the saucepan, then boil until the mixture thickens. Stir in the remaining cherries, pour into the pastry shell, then dot with the melted butter. Cut the remaining dough into strips ½ inch wide. Lay the strips over the filling, crossing to form a lattice. Trim and seal the edges with water. Use your fingers to crimp around the rim, then glaze the top with the beaten egg.

3 Cover the pie with aluminum foil and bake for 30 minutes in the oven. Remove from the oven, discard the foil, and bake for another 15 minutes, or until golden. Serve with ice cream.

★ Variation

Add cranberries to the filling for extra flavor.

BEST BAKED SNACKS AND BREADS

VANILLA CUPCAKES

Makes: 12

Prep: 30 minutes,
plus cooling

Cook: 15–20 minutes

Ingredients

1½ sticks unsalted butter, softened

¾ cup superfine or granulated sugar

3 extra-large eggs, beaten

1 teaspoon vanilla extract

1⅓ cups all-purpose flour

1¼ teaspoons baking powder

Frosting

1¼ sticks unsalted butter, softened

3 tablespoons heavy cream or milk

1 teaspoon vanilla extract

2⅓ cups confectioners' sugar, sifted

sprinkles, to decorate

Method

1 Preheat the oven to 350°F. Put 12 paper cupcake liners into a cupcake pan.

2 Put the butter and superfine sugar into a bowl and whisk beat until pale and creamy. Gradually beat in the eggs and vanilla extract. Sift in the flour and baking powder and fold in gently.

3 Divide the batter evenly among the paper liners and bake in the preheated oven for 15–20 minutes, or until risen and firm to the touch. Transfer to a wire rack and let cool.

4 To make the frosting, put the butter into a bowl and beat with an electric mixer for 2–3 minutes, or until pale and creamy. Beat in the cream and vanilla extract. Gradually beat in the confectioners' sugar and continue beating until the buttercream is light and fluffy.

5 Use a spatula to swirl the frosting over the tops of the cupcakes, then decorate with the sprinkles.

★ **Variation**

To make bite-size cupcakes for children's parties, divide the batter among 30 mini cupcake liners and reduce the cooking time to 8–10 minutes.

CHERRY CAKE

Serves: 8

Prep: 30 minutes, plus cooling

Cook: 1–1¼ hours

Ingredients

1¼ cups quartered candied cherries

¾ cup ground almonds (almond meal)

1⅔ cups all-purpose flour

1 teaspoon baking powder

1¾ sticks unsalted butter, plus extra for greasing

1 cup superfine or granulated sugar

3 extra-large eggs

finely grated zest and juice of 1 lemon

6 sugar cubes, crushed

Method

1 Preheat the oven to 350°F. Grease an 8-inch round cake pan and line with parchment paper.

2 Stir together the cherries, ground almonds, and 1 tablespoon of the flour. Sift together the remaining flour and the baking powder into a separate bowl.

3 Cream together the butter and sugar until light and fluffy. Gradually add the eggs, beating hard, until evenly mixed.

4 Add the flour mixture and fold lightly and evenly into the creamed mixture, using a metal spoon. Add the cherry mixture, fold in evenly, then fold in the lemon zest and juice.

5 Spoon the batter into the prepared pan and sprinkle with the crushed sugar cubes. Bake in the preheated oven for 1–1¼ hours, or until risen and golden brown and shrinking from the sides of the pan.

6 Let cool in the pan for about 15 minutes, then turn out onto a wire rack to cool completely.

LAVENDER SHORTBREAD

Serves: 8

Prep: 25–30 minutes,   Cook: 30–35 minutes
plus chilling and cooling

Ingredients

1 stick butter, softened,
plus extra for greasing

¼ cup lavender superfine
or granulated sugar*, plus
extra for sprinkling

1¼ cups all-purpose flour

3 tablespoons cornstarch

(*Note: To make lavender
sugar, mix 1 tablespoon
fresh lavender flowers or
1 teaspoon dried lavender
flowers with 1 cup sugar of
your choice in an air-tight
container. Seal and store
in a cool, dark place for
1 week to let the flavors
develop.)

Method

1 Preheat the oven to 325°F. Lightly grease a baking
sheet. Put the butter into a mixing bowl. Sift the
sugar over the butter (reserving the lavender
flowers left in the sifter) and beat together with
a wooden spoon until light and fluffy.

2 Sift the flour and cornstarch over the butter
mixture and add the reserved lavender flowers.
Gradually work the flour and cornstarch into
the creamed mixture to form a crumbly dough.
Gather the dough together with your hands
and knead lightly until smooth. Wrap the dough
in plastic wrap and chill in the refrigerator for
20 minutes.

3 Put the dough on the baking sheet and, using
clean hands, press it out to a 7-inch circle.
Smooth the top by gently rolling a rolling pin
over the mixture a couple of times. Crimp
around the edge and mark into eight triangles
with a sharp knife. Sprinkle with a little more
lavender sugar. Chill in the refrigerator for at least
30 minutes, until firm. Bake in the preheated oven
for 30–35 minutes, until just pale golden. Let the
shortbread cool on the sheet for 10 minutes, then
transfer to a wire rack to cool completely.

SCONES

Makes: 12

Prep: 25 minutes, plus cooling

Cook: 10–12 minutes

Ingredients

3 ⅔ cups all-purpose flour, plus extra for dusting

½ teaspoon salt

2 teaspoons baking powder

4 tablespoons butter

2 tablespoons sugar

1 cup milk

3 tablespoons milk, for glazing

strawberry preserves and clotted cream*, to serve

(*Note: To make a clotted cream subsitute, whip 1 cup mascarpone cheese with ⅓ cup heavy cream until thick, then chill until ready to use.)

Method

1 Preheat the oven to 425°F. Lightly flour or line a baking sheet with parchment paper.

2 Sift the flour, salt, and baking powder into a bowl. Rub in the butter until the mixture resembles bread crumbs. Stir in the sugar. Make a well in the center and pour in the milk. Stir in, using a blunt knife, and make a soft dough.

3 Turn the dough onto a floured surface and lightly flatten until it is of an even thickness, about ½ inch. Don't be heavy handed; scones need a light touch.

4 Use a 2½-inch pastry cutter to cut out the scones, and place them on the prepared baking sheet. Glaze with a little milk and bake in the preheated oven for 10–12 minutes, until golden and well risen. Cool on a wire rack and serve freshly baked, with strawberry preserves and clotted cream.

RHUBARB, RAISIN & GINGER MUFFINS

Makes: 12

Prep: 25 minutes, plus cooling

Cook: 20–25 minutes

Ingredients

oil or melted butter, for greasing (if using)

5 rhubarb stalks (about 2 cups prepared)

1⅔ cups all-purpose flour

2 teaspoons baking powder

⅔ cup superfine or granulated sugar

2 eggs

½ cup milk

1 stick butter, melted and cooled

3 tablespoons raisins

2 pieces of preserved ginger in syrup, drained and chopped

Method

1 Preheat the oven to 350°F. Grease a 12-cup muffin pan or line with 12 paper muffin cups. Chop the rhubarb into ½ -inch lengths.

2 Sift together the flour and baking powder into a large bowl. Stir in the sugar. Lightly beat the eggs in a small bowl, then beat in the milk and melted butter. Make a well in the center of the dry ingredients and pour in the beaten liquid ingredients. Stir in the rhubarb, raisins, and preserved ginger until just combined; do not overmix.

3 Spoon the batter into the prepared muffin pan. Bake in the preheated oven for 15–20 minutes, until well risen, golden brown, and firm to the touch.

4 Let the muffins cool in the pan for 5 minutes, then serve warm or transfer to a wire rack and let cool.

CLASSIC OATMEAL COOKIES

Makes: 30

Prep: 20–25 minutes, Cook: 15 minutes
plus cooling

Ingredients

1½ sticks butter, softened, plus extra for greasing

1⅓ cups firmly packed light brown sugar

1 egg, beaten

¼ cup water

1 teaspoon vanilla extract

4 cups rolled oats

1 cup plus 2 tablespoons all-purpose flour

1 teaspoon salt

½ teaspoon baking soda

Method

1 Preheat the oven to 350°F. Grease two large baking sheets.

2 Put the butter and sugar into a large bowl and beat together until pale and creamy. Beat in the egg, water, and vanilla extract until the mixture is smooth. Mix the oats, flour, salt, and baking soda together in a separate bowl, then gradually stir the oat mixture into the creamed mixture until thoroughly combined.

3 Place tablespoonfuls of the dough on the prepared baking sheets, spaced well apart.

4 Bake in the preheated oven for 15 minutes, or until golden brown. Transfer to a wire rack to cool completely.

GINGERSNAPS

Makes: 30

Prep: 25–30 minutes,   Cook: 20–25 minutes
plus cooling

Ingredients

2¾ cups all-purpose flour

2¾ teaspoons
baking powder

pinch of salt

1 cup superfine or
granulated sugar

tablespoon ground ginger

1 teaspoon baking soda

1 stick butter,
plus extra for greasing

⅓ cup light corn syrup

1 egg, beaten

1 teaspoon grated
orange zest

Method

1 Preheat the oven to 325°F. Lightly grease several baking sheets.

2 Sift together the flour, baking powder, salt, sugar, ginger, and baking soda into a large mixing bowl.

3 Heat the butter and light corn syrup together in a saucepan over low heat until the butter has melted. Remove the pan from the heat and let cool slightly, then pour the contents onto the dry ingredients.

4 Add the egg and orange zest to the flour mixture and mix thoroughly, using a wooden spoon, to form a dough. Using your hands, carefully shape the dough into 30 even balls. Put the balls onto the prepared baking sheets, spaced well apart, then flatten them slightly with your fingers.

5 Bake in the preheated oven for 15–20 minutes, then carefully transfer to a wire rack to cool completely.

BEST BAKED SNACKS AND BREADS

ICED LEMON CAKE

Serves: 10

Prep: 35 minutes, plus cooling and setting

Cook: 1–1¼ hours

Ingredients

1½ sticks unsalted butter, softened, plus extra for greasing

¾ cup plus 2 tablespoons superfine or granulated sugar

finely grated zest of 1 lemon

3 eggs, lightly beaten

2 cups all-purpose flour

1 teaspoon baking powder

2 tablespoons milk

1 tablespoon lemon juice

Icing

1⅓ cups confectioners' sugar

2–3 tablespoons lemon juice

2 teaspoons lemon curd, warmed

Method

1 Preheat the oven to 325°F. Grease a 9 x 5 x 3-inch loaf pan and line with parchment paper.

2 Put the butter and superfine sugar into a large bowl and beat together until pale and fluffy. Beat in the lemon zest then gradually beat in the eggs.

3 Sift the all-purpose flour and baking powder into the mixture and fold in gently until thoroughly incorporated. Fold in the milk and lemon juice.

4 Spoon the batter into the prepared pan and bake in the preheated oven for 1–1¼ hours, or until well risen, golden brown, and a toothpick inserted into the center comes out clean. Cool in the pan for 15 minutes, then turn out onto a wire rack to cool completely.

5 For the icing, sift the confectioners' sugar into a bowl. Add the lemon juice and stir to make a smooth and thick icing. Gently spread the icing over the top of the cake. Drizzle the warmed lemon curd over the icing and drag a toothpick through the icing to create a swirled effect. Let set.

IRISH SPICED FRUITCAKE

Serves: 8–10

Prep: 25 minutes, plus cooling

Cook: 2 hours, 10 minutes

Ingredients

1¼ cups mixed dried fruit, such as golden raisins, dried currants, and raisins

⅔ cupz dried unsweetened cherries

⅓ cup coarsely chopped walnuts

¾ cup firmly packed dark brown sugar

1 stick butter, plus extra for greasing

1 teaspoon allspice

1 teaspoon ground ginger

½ teaspoon baking soda

1 cup milk

1¾ cups all-purpose flour

1¾ teaspoons baking powder

2 eggs, lightly beaten

Method

1 Put all the ingredients apart from the flour, baking powder, and eggs into a saucepan and mix well. Bring to a boil over medium–high heat, stirring constantly. Reduce the heat slightly and simmer for 5 minutes, stirring occasionally. Remove from the heat and let cool for about 30 minutes.

2 Meanwhile, preheat the oven to 350°F. Grease and line a deep 8-inch cake pan.

3 Add the flour, baking powder, and eggs to the cake mixture, mixing well to combine. Spoon the batter into the prepared pan, leveling the surface with a wet spatula.

4 Bake in the preheated oven for 30 minutes. Reduce the oven temperature to 325°F and bake for an additional 1½ hours, or until a toothpick inserted in the center comes out clean.

5 Let the cake to cool in the pan for 10 minutes, then turn out onto a wire rack and let cool completely.

CUSTARD TARTS

Serves: 12

Prep: 40–45 minutes,   Cook: 30 minutes
plus cooling

Ingredients

butter, for greasing

5 egg yolks, lightly beaten

½ cup superfine or
granulated sugar

2 teaspoons cornstarch

½ cup milk

1 cup heavy cream

2-inch cinnamon stick

2 strips orange peel

½ teaspoon vanilla extract

1 sheet ready-to-bake
puff pastry

freshly grated nutmeg,
for sprinkling

flour, for dusting

Method

1 Preheat the oven to 375°F. Lightly grease a
12-cup muffin pan. Combine the egg yolks and
sugar in a mixing bowl. Stir in the cornstarch and
mix to a smooth paste, then whisk in the milk.

2 Heat the cream in a heavy saucepan until just
starting to simmer but not boiling. Gradually
whisk the hot cream into the egg mixture, then
return the mixture to the pan. Add the cinnamon
stick and orange peel. Whisk constantly
over medium heat for about 5 minutes, until
thickened. Immediately pour into a small bowl.
Stir in the vanilla extract. Cover with plastic wrap
to prevent a skin from forming and set aside.

3 Place the sheet of puff pastry on a board
and trim to a rectangle measuring about
11 x 9½ inches. Discard the scraps or use in
another recipe. Slice in half lengthwise to make
two rectangles, each measuring 11 x 4½ inches.
Sprinkle one rectangle with freshly grated
nutmeg. Place the other on top to make a
sandwich. Roll up from the narrow end to
make a log. Using a sharp knife, cut the log
into twelve ½-inch slices.

4 Roll out the slices on a floured board to 4½-inch circles. Put the circles into the muffin pan cups, lightly pressing down into the bottom and leaving a slightly thicker rim around the top edge.

5 Remove the cinnamon stick and orange peel from the custard and discard. Pour the custard into the pastry shells.

6 Bake for 20 minutes, or until the pastry and filling are golden brown. Let the tarts cool in the pan for 5 minutes, then transfer to a wire rack to cool.

COFFEE & WALNUT CAKE

Serves: 8

Prep: 35 minutes, plus cooling

Cook: 20–25 minutes

Ingredients

1½ sticks unsalted butter, softened, plus extra for greasing

¾ cup firmly packed light brown sugar

3 extra-large eggs, beaten

3 tablespoons strong black coffee

1⅓ cups all-purpose flour

2½ teaspoons baking powder

1 cup walnut pieces

walnut halves, to decorate

Frosting

1 stick unsalted butter, softened

1⅔ cups confectioners' sugar

1 tablespoon strong black coffee

½ teaspoon vanilla extract

Method

1 Preheat the oven to 350°F. Grease two 8-inch cake pans and line with parchment paper.

2 Beat the butter and brown sugar together until pale and creamy. Gradually add the eggs, beating well after each addition. Beat in the coffee.

3 Sift the flour and baking powder into the mixture, then fold in lightly and evenly, using a metal spoon. Fold in the walnut pieces. Divide the batter between the prepared cake pans and smooth the surfaces. Bake in the preheated oven for 20–25 minutes, or until golden brown and springy to the touch. Turn out onto a wire rack to cool completely.

4 To make the frosting, beat together the butter, confectioners' sugar, coffee, and vanilla extract, mixing until smooth and creamy.

5 Use about half the frosting to sandwich the cakes together, then spread the remaining frosting on top and swirl with a spatula. Decorate with walnut halves.

RASPBERRY CRUMB MUFFINS

Makes: 12

Prep: 25 minutes,
plus cooling

Cook: 25 minutes

Ingredients

2¼ cups all-purpose flour

1 tablespoon baking powder

½ teaspoon baking soda

pinch of salt

½ cup granulated sugar

2 eggs

1 cup plain yogurt

6 tablespoons butter, melted and cooled, plus extra for greasing

1 teaspoon vanilla extract

1 cup frozen raspberries

crumb topping

⅓ cup all-purpose flour

2 tablespoons butter

2 tablespoons sugar

Method

1 Preheat the oven to 400°F. Grease a 12-cup muffin pan or line with 12 paper muffin cups.

2 To make the crumb topping, sift the flour into a bowl. Cut the butter into small pieces, add to the bowl with the flour, and rub it in with your fingertips until the mixture resembles fine bread crumbs. Stir in the sugar and set aside.

3 To make the muffins, sift together the flour, baking powder, baking soda, and salt into a large bowl. Stir in the sugar.

4 Lightly whisk the eggs in a large bowl, then whisk in the yogurt, butter, and vanilla extract. Make a well in the center of the dry ingredients, pour in the beaten liquid ingredients, and add the raspberries. Stir gently until just combined. Do not overmix.

5 Spoon the batter into the prepared pan. Sprinkle the crumb topping over each muffin and press down lightly. Bake in the preheated oven for about 20 minutes, until well risen, golden brown, and firm to the touch.

6 Let the muffins cool in the pan for 5 minutes, then serve warm or transfer to a wire rack to cool completely.

BEST BAKED SNACKS AND BREADS

CHOCOLATE CARAMEL SHORTBREAD

Makes: 12

Prep: 25–30 minutes,   Cook: 25–30 minutes
plus chilling

Ingredients

1 stick butter,
plus extra for greasing

1⅓ cups all-purpose flour

¼ cup superfine or
granulated sugar

Filling and topping

1½ sticks butter

½ cup superfine or
granulated sugar

3 tablespoons
light corn syrup

1 (14-ounce) can
sweetened condensed milk

8 ounces semisweet
chocolate, broken
into pieces

Method

1 Preheat the oven to 350°F. Grease and line a shallow 9-inch square cake pan with parchment paper.

2 Put the butter, flour, and sugar into a food processor and process until it begins to bind together. Press the dough into the prepared pan and smooth the top. Bake in the preheated oven for 20–25 minutes.

3 Meanwhile, make the filling. Put the butter, sugar, light corn syrup, and condensed milk into a saucepan and heat gently until the sugar has dissolved. Bring to a boil and simmer for 6–8 minutes, stirring constantly, until the mixture becomes thick. Pour over the shortbread crust and let chill in the refrigerator until firm.

4 To make the topping, put the chocolate into a heatproof bowl, set the bowl over a saucepan of gently simmering water, and heat until melted, then spread it over the caramel. Chill in the refrigerator until set. Cut the shortbread into 12 pieces with a sharp knife and serve.

LEMON BUTTERFLY CUPCAKES

Makes: 12

Prep: 30 minutes, plus cooling

Cook: 15–20 minutes

Ingredients

1 cup all-purpose flour

1½ teaspoons baking powder

1 stick butter, softened

½ cup superfine or granulated sugar

2 eggs, beaten

finely grated zest of ¾ lemon

2–4 tablespoons milk

confectioners' sugar, for dusting

Filling

4 tablespoons butter

1 cup confectioners' sugar

1 tablespoon lemon juice

Method

1 Preheat the oven to 375°F. Put 12 paper cupcake liners into a cupcake pan.

2 Sift the flour and baking powder into a bowl. Add the butter, superfine sugar, eggs, lemon zest, and enough milk to produce a medium-soft consistency. Beat the mixture thoroughly until smooth, then divide among the paper liners.

3 Bake in the preheated oven for 15–20 minutes, or until well risen and golden. Transfer to a wire rack to cool.

4 To make the filling, put the butter into a bowl. Sift in the confectioners' sugar and add the lemon juice. Beat well until smooth and creamy.

5 When the cakes are completely cooled, use a small sharp knife to cut a circle from the top of each cake, then cut each circle in half. Spoon a little buttercream on top of each cake and press the two semicircular pieces into it to resemble wings. Dust the cakes with confectioners' sugar before serving.

CHOCOLATE & CHERRY BROWNIES

Makes: 12　　　**Prep: 25 minutes,** plus cooling　　　**Cook: 50–55 minutes**

Ingredients

6 ounces semisweet
chocolate, broken into pieces

1½ sticks butter,
plus extra for greasing

cup superfine or granulated
sugar

3 extra-large eggs, beaten

1 teaspoon vanilla extract

1 cup all-purpose flour

1 teaspoon baking powder

1 cup pitted fresh cherries

3 ounces white chocolate,
coarsely chopped

Method

1 Preheat the oven to 350°F. Grease a shallow
9½ x 8-inch baking pan, then line it with
parchment paper.

2 Put the semisweet chocolate and butter into a
large, heatproof bowl set over a saucepan of
simmering water and heat until melted. Remove
from the heat and let cool for 5 minutes.

3 Beat the sugar, eggs, and vanilla extract into the
chocolate mixture. Sift in the flour and baking
powder, then fold in gently. Pour the batter into
the prepared pan. Sprinkle with the cherries and
chopped white chocolate.

4 Bake in the preheated oven for 30 minutes.
Loosely cover the tops of the brownies with
aluminum foil and bake for an additional
15–20 minutes, or until just firm to the touch.
Let cool in the pan, then cut into pieces.

BEST BAKED SNACKS AND BREADS

DATE & WALNUT LOAF

Serves: 8

Prep: 25 minutes, **Cook: 35–40 minutes**
plus soaking and cooling

Ingredients

⅔ cup pitted and chopped dates

½ teaspoon baking soda

finely grated zest of ½ lemon

½ cup hot tea

3 tablespoons unsalted butter, plus extra for greasing

⅓ cup firmly packed light brown sugar

1 medium egg

1 cup all-purpose flour

1 teaspoon baking powder

¼ cup chopped walnuts

walnut halves, to decorate

Method

1 Preheat the oven to 350°F. Grease an 8½ x 4½ x 2½-inch loaf pan and line with parchment paper.

2 Put the dates, baking soda, and lemon zest into a bowl and add the hot tea. Let soak for 10 minutes, until softened.

3 Cream the butter and sugar together until light and fluffy, then beat in the egg. Stir in the date mixture.

4 Sift the flour and baking powder over the butter mixture, fold in, using a large metal spoon, then fold in the walnuts. Spoon the batter into the prepared loaf pan and smooth the surface. Top with the walnut halves.

5 Bake in the preheated oven for 35–40 minutes or until risen, firm, and golden brown. Cool for 10 minutes in the pan, then turn out onto a wire rack to cool completely.

WHOLE WHEAT MUFFINS

Makes: 10

Prep: 25 minutes,
plus cooling

Cook: 25–30 minutes

Ingredients

1¾ cups whole wheat flour

3¾ teaspoons
baking powder

2 tablespoons packed
light brown sugar

⅔ cup finely chopped
dried apricots

1 banana, mashed with
1 tablespoon orange juice

1 teaspoon orange zest,
finely grated

1¼ cups skim milk

1 egg, beaten

3 tablespoons vegetable oil

2 tablespoons rolled oats

fruit spread, honey, or
maple syrup, to serve

Method

1 Preheat the oven to 400°F. Put 10 paper muffin cups into a muffin pan. Sift the flour and baking powder into a mixing bowl, adding any husks that remain in the sifter. Stir in the sugar and chopped apricots.

2 Make a well in the center of the dry ingredients and add the banana, orange zest, milk, beaten egg, and oil. Mix together well to form a thick batter. Divide the batter evenly among the 10 paper liners.

3 Sprinkle each muffin with a few rolled oats and bake in the preheated oven for 25–30 minutes, or until well risen and firm to the touch. Transfer to a wire rack to cool slightly. Serve the muffins warm with a little fruit spread, honey, or maple syrup.

IRISH FRUITCAKE

Makes: one 7-inch cake

Prep: 35 minutes, plus soaking, cooling, and storing

Cook: 2 ¼–3 hours

Ingredients

2½ cups mixed dried currants and golden raisins

¾ cup dried unsweetened cherries

⅔ cup finely chopped candied peel

1⅓ cups stout

2¾ cups all-purpose flour

1 teaspoon baking powder

1 teaspoon allspice

pinch of salt

2 sticks butter, plus extra for greasing

1 cup firmly packed brown sugar

3 eggs, lightly beaten

Method

1 Mix the currants, golden raisins, cherries, and candied peel in a large bowl. Add the stout and let soak for at least 5 hours or overnight, stirring occasionally.

2 Preheat the oven to 325°F. Grease and line a 7-inch square cake pan. Sift the flour, baking powder, allspice, and salt into a large bowl.

3 Cream the butter and sugar in a separate bowl for about 4 minutes, until light and fluffy. Stir in the beaten eggs, a little at a time, adding some of the flour mixture at each addition and beating well. Stir in the remaining flour.

4 Add the fruit and any liquid to the mixture, mixing well to a soft consistency. Spoon the batter into the prepared pan, leveling the surface with a wet spatula.

5 Bake in the preheated oven for 1 hour. Reduce the oven temperature to 300°F and bake for an additional 1½–2 hours, or until a toothpick inserted in the center comes out clean. Let stand in the pan until completely cool.

6 Turn out, wrap in wax paper, and store in an airtight container.

CORNBREAD

Makes: 1 loaf

Prep: 25 minutes,
plus cooling

Cook: 30–35 minutes

Ingredients

vegetable oil, for greasing

1⅓ cups all-purpose flour

1 teaspoon salt

4 teaspoons baking powder

1 teaspoon sugar

2 cups cornmeal

1 stick butter, softened

4 eggs

1 cup milk

3 tablespoons heavy cream

Method

1 Preheat the oven to 400°F. Brush an 8-inch square cake pan with oil.

2 Sift together the flour, salt, and baking powder into a bowl. Add the sugar and cornmeal and stir to mix. Add the butter and cut into the dry ingredients with a knife, then rub it in with your fingertips until the mixture resembles fine bread crumbs.

3 Lightly beat the eggs in a bowl with the milk and cream, then stir into the cornmeal mixture until thoroughly combined.

4 Spoon the batter into the prepared pan and smooth the surface. Bake in the preheated oven for 30–35 minutes, until a wooden toothpick inserted into the center of the loaf comes out clean. Remove the pan from the oven and let cool for 5–10 minutes, then cut into squares and serve warm.

ENGLISH MUFFINS

Makes: 10–12

Prep: 35–40 minutes, plus rising and optional cooling

Cook: 30–35 minutes

Ingredients

3¼ cups white bread flour, plus extra for dusting

½ teaspoon salt

1 teaspoon sugar

1½ teaspoons active dry yeast

1 cup lukewarm water

½ cup plain yogurt

vegetable oil, for oiling

¼ cup coarse ground cornmeal

butter and jelly or preserves, to serve

Method

1 Sift the flour and salt together into a bowl and stir in the sugar and yeast. Make a well in the center and add the water and yogurt. Stir with a wooden spoon until the dough begins to come together, then knead with your hands until it comes away from the side of the bowl. Turn out onto a lightly floured surface and knead for 5–10 minutes, until smooth and elastic.

2 Brush a bowl with oil. Shape the dough into a ball, put it in the bowl, and cover with a damp dish towel. Let rise in a warm place for 30–40 minutes, until the dough doubles in volume. Dust a baking sheet with flour. Turn out the dough onto a lightly floured surface and knead lightly. Roll out to a thickness of ¾ inch. Stamp out 10–12 circles with a 3-inch cookie cutter and sprinkle each circle with cornmeal. Place on the baking sheet, cover with a damp dish towel, and let rise in a warm place for 30–40 minutes.

4 Heat a flat griddle pan or large skillet over medium-high heat and brush lightly with oil. Add half the muffins and cook for 7–8 minutes on each side, until golden brown. Cook the remaining muffins in the same way. Serve hot with butter and jelly or let cool, then halve and toast them before serving.

★ Variation

Add fresh blueberries or raspberries as preferred.

BROWN SODA BREAD WITH MOLASSES

Makes: 1 loaf

Prep: 20 minutes,
plus cooling

Cook: 35–40 minutes

Ingredients

2 cups all-purpose flour,
plus extra for dusting

2 cups whole wheat flour

1 cup jumbo rolled oats

1½ teaspoons salt

1 teaspoon baking soda

1¾ cups buttermilk

2 tablespoons molasses

Method

1 Preheat the oven to 450°F. Line a baking sheet with a sheet of nonstick parchment paper.

2 Combine the flours, oats, salt, and baking soda in a large bowl, mixing thoroughly.

3 Whisk together the buttermilk and molasses in a small bowl. Make a well in the center of the flour mixture and pour in the buttermilk mixture. Using a fork, stir the liquid, gradually drawing in the flour from around the edge. With floured hands, lightly knead to a soft dough.

4 Shape the dough into a circle and place on the lined baking sheet. Press flat to about 2 inches thick. Use a sharp knife with a long blade to cut a deep cross on the top.

5 Bake in the preheated oven for 15 minutes, then reduce the oven temperature to 400°F. Bake for an additional 20–25 minutes, or until the bottom of the bread sounds hollow when tapped. Transfer to a wire rack and let cool slightly. Serve warm.

MOLASSES BREAD

Makes: 1 loaf

Prep: 30 minutes,
plus cooling

Cook: 45–55 minutes

Ingredients

1¾ cups all-purpose flour

1 teaspoon baking soda

½ teaspoon allspice

½ teaspoon ground ginger

4 tablespoons salted butter,
plus extra for greasing
and to serve

3 tablespoons molasses

2 eggs, lightly beaten

⅓ cup buttermilk

¼ cup firmly packed
dark brown sugar

¼ cup dried currants

⅓ cup golden raisins

Method

1 Preheat the oven to 350°F. Grease and line a small 6½ x 3¼-inch loaf pan.

2 Sift the flour, baking soda, and spices into a bowl. Lightly rub in the butter until the mixture resembles fine bread crumbs.

3 Whisk the molasses with the eggs and buttermilk, then stir in the sugar. Make a well in the center of the flour mixture and pour in the molasses mixture. Mix with a fork, gradually drawing in the flour from around the edges.

4 Add the currants and golden raisins, and mix to a soft dough. Spoon the dough into the prepared loaf pan, leveling the surface with a wet spatula.

5 Bake in the preheated oven for 45–55 minutes, or until a toothpick inserted in the center comes out clean.

6 Let cool in the pan for 15 minutes, then turn out onto a wire rack and let stand for about 2 hours to cool completely.

7 Serve spread thickly with butter.

Makes: 12–14

Prep: 25–30 minutes,   Cook: 12–15 minutes
plus cooling

Ingredients

1 stock unsalted butter, plus extra for greasing

1 cup rolled oats

3 tablespoons whole wheat flour

½ teaspoon coarse sea salt

1 teaspoon dried thyme

⅓ cup finely chopped walnuts

1 egg, beaten

¼ cup sesame seeds

Method

1 Preheat the oven to 350°F. Lightly grease two baking sheets.

2 Rub the butter into the oats and flour, using your fingertips. Stir in the salt, thyme, and walnuts, then add the egg and mix to a soft dough. Spread out the sesame seeds on a large, shallow plate. Break off walnut-size pieces of dough and roll into balls, then roll in the sesame seeds to coat lightly and evenly.

3 Place the balls of dough on the prepared baking sheets, spaced well apart, and roll a rolling pin over them to flatten. Bake in the preheated oven for 12–15 minutes, or until firm and pale golden. Transfer to a wire rack and let cool.

SEEDED BREAD ROLLS

Makes: 8

Prep: 30 minutes,
plus rising and cooling

Cook: 10–15 minutes

Ingredients

3⅓ cups white bread flour,
plus extra for dusting

1 teaspoon salt

2¼ teaspoons
active dry yeast

1 tablespoon vegetable oil,
plus extra for brushing

1½ cups lukewarm water

1 egg, beaten

sesame or poppy seeds,
for sprinkling

Method

1 Put the flour, salt, and yeast into a large bowl and mix well. Pour in the oil and add the water, then mix well to make a smooth dough.

2 Turn out onto a lightly floured surface and knead well for 5–7 minutes, or until smooth and elastic. Brush a bowl with oil. Shape the dough into a ball, put it into the bowl, and cover with a damp dish towel. Let rise in a warm place for 1 hour, or until the dough has doubled in volume.

3 Turn out the dough onto a lightly floured surface and knead briefly until smooth. Divide the dough into eight pieces. Shape the dough into round rolls. Place the rolls on a baking sheet.

4 Cover the rolls with a damp dish towel and let rise for 30 minutes, or until the rolls have doubled in size.

5 Preheat the oven to 425°F. Brush the rolls with the beaten egg and sprinkle with the seeds. Bake in the preheated oven for 10–15 minutes, or until golden brown. Test that the rolls are cooked by tapping on the bottoms with your knuckles; they should sound hollow. Transfer to a wire rack to cool.

MALTED WHEAT LOAF

Makes: 1 loaf

Prep: 25 minutes,
plus rising and cooling

Cook: 30–35 minutes

Ingredients

flour mixture

2½ cups all-purpose flour, plus extra for dusting

⅔ cup whole wheat flour

⅔ cup malted wheat flakes (available online)

3 tablespoons malt powder

1½ teaspoons salt

2 teaspoons active dry yeast

2 teaspoons sunflower seeds

1 tablespoon sunflower oil, plus extra for greasing

1 teaspoon honey

1¼ cups lukewarm water

Method

1 Mix the flours, wheat flakes, and malt powder to make 4 cups of a malted wheat flour mixture. Add the salt, yeast, and sunflower seeds to the flour mixture, mix together, and make a well in the center. Mix together the oil, honey, and warm water and pour into the bowl. Mix with a knife to make a soft, sticky dough.

2 Turn the dough onto a floured surface and knead for 10 minutes, until smooth and elastic, adding a little more all-purpose flour if the dough becomes too sticky. Put into a bowl, cover with lightly oiled plastic wrap, and let rest in a warm place for 1–1½ hours, until doubled in size. Preheat the oven to 425°F. Lightly grease a 9 x 5 x 3-inch loaf pan.

3 Turn out the dough onto a floured surface and knead again lightly for 1 minute. Shape into an oblong and place in the loaf pan. Cover with a clean, damp dish towel and let rest in a warm place for about 30 minutes, until the dough has risen above the top edges of the pan.

4 Dust the top of the loaf lightly with flour. Bake in the preheated oven for 30–35 minutes, until golden brown and the loaf sounds hollow when tapped on the bottom with your knuckles. Transfer to a wire rack to cool.

SEEDED RYE BREAD

Makes: 1 loaf

Prep: 25–30 minutes, Cook: 35–40 minutes
plus rising and cooling

Ingredients

1½ cups rye flour, plus extra for dusting

2 cups white bread flour

1½ teaspoon salt

1 tablespoon caraway seeds

2¼ teaspoons active dry yeast

2 tablespoons butter, melted

2 tablespoons honey, warmed

1¼ cups lukewarm water

sunflower oil, for greasing

Method

1 Mix the rye flour, white flour, salt, caraway seeds, and yeast in a large bowl and make a well in the center. Mix together the butter, honey, and water and pour into the well. Mix with a knife to make a soft, sticky dough. Lightly grease a baking sheet with oil.

2 Turn out the dough onto a floured work surface and knead for 10 minutes, or until smooth and elastic. Shape into an oval and place on the prepared baking sheet. Slash the top of the loaf in a diamond pattern, lightly dust with flour, and let rest in a warm place for 1–1½ hours, or until doubled in size.

3 Meanwhile, preheat the oven to 375°F. Bake in the preheated oven for 30–35 minutes, or until the crust is a rich brown and the bottom of the loaf sounds hollow when tapped with your knuckles. Transfer to a wire rack to cool.

OAT & POTATO BREAD

Makes: 1 loaf

Prep: 30-35 minutes,   Cook: 50-60 minutes
plus cooling and rising

Ingredients

vegetable oil, for oiling

2 russet potatoes

3⅔ cups white bread flour,
plus extra for dusting

1½ teaspoons salt

3 tablespoons butter, diced

1½ teaspoons active dry yeast

1½ tablespoons firmly packed
dark brown sugar

3 tablespoons rolled oats

2 tablespoons instant dry milk

1 cup lukewarm water

Topping

1 tablespoon water

1 tablespoon rolled oats

Method

1 Oil a 9 x 5 x 3-inch loaf pan. Put the potatoes into a large saucepan, add water to cover, and bring to a boil. Cook for 20–25 minutes, until tender. Drain, then mash until smooth. Let cool.

2 Sift the flour and salt into a warm bowl. Rub in the butter with your fingertips. Stir in the yeast, sugar, oats, and dry milk. Mix in the mashed potatoes, then add the water and mix to a soft dough. Turn out the dough onto a lightly floured work surface and knead for 5–10 minutes, or until smooth and elastic. Put the dough into an oiled bowl, cover with plastic wrap, and let rise in a warm place for 1 hour, or until doubled in size.

3 Turn out the dough again and knead lightly. Shape into a loaf and transfer to the prepared pan. Cover and let rise in a warm place for 30 minutes. Meanwhile, preheat the oven to 425°F.

4 Brush the surface of the loaf with the water and carefully sprinkle with the oats. Bake in the preheated oven for 25–30 minutes, or until it sounds hollow when tapped on the bottom. Transfer to a wire rack and let cool slightly. Serve warm.

★ Variation

Spread mayonnaise on slices, then top with smoked salmon and a squeeze of lemon juice.

INDEX

This edition published by Parragon Books Ltd in 2015
and distributed by

Parragon Inc.
440 Park Avenue South, 13th Floor
New York, NY 10016
www.parragon.com/lovefood

LOVE FOOD is an imprint of Parragon Books Ltd

Copyright © Parragon Books Ltd 2015

LOVE FOOD and the accompanying heart device is a registered
trademark of Parragon Books Ltd in the USA, the UK, Australia, India, and
the EU.

All rights reserved. No part of this publication may be reproduced,
stored in a retrieval system, or transmitted, in any form or by any means,
electric, mechanical, photocopying, recording, or otherwise, without
the prior permission of the copyright holder.

ISBN 978-1-4723-9304-3
Printed in China

Introduction by Robin Donovan
Front and back cover photography by Ian Garlick.
Cover food stylist Nikki Gee

Notes for the Reader
This book uses standard kitchen measuring spoons and cups. All spoon
and cup measurements are level unless otherwise indicated. Unless
otherwise stated, milk is assumed to be whole, eggs are large, individual
vegetables are medium, and pepper is freshly ground black pepper.
Unless otherwise stated, all root vegetables should be peeled prior
to using.

Garnishes, decorations, and serving suggestions are all optional and
not necessarily included in the recipe ingredients or method. The
times given are only an approximate guide. Preparation times differ
according to the techniques used by different people and the cooking
times may also vary from those given. Optional ingredients, variations, or
serving suggestions have not been included in the time calculations.

For the front cover recipe, please see page 8.
For the back cover recipe, please see page 242 .